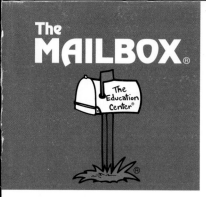

The MAILBOX®

Songs, Poems and Fingerplays

grades PreK–K

THE BEST OF The MAILBOX® MAGAZINE

The best songs, poems, and fingerplays from the 1997–2004 issues of The Mailbox® magazine!

- **Fall**
- **Winter**
- **Spring**
- **Summer**
- **Basic Concepts**
- **Daily Routines**
- **Movement**
- **Favorite Themes**

And Much, Much More!

Over 300 Songs, Poems, and Fingerplays!

Editorial Team: Becky S. Andrews, Kimberley Bruck, Karen P. Shelton, Diane Badden, Thad H. McLaurin, Sharon Murphy, Karen A. Brudnak, Hope Rodgers, Dorothy C. McKinney

Production Team: Lori Z. Henry, Pam Crane, Rebecca Saunders, Jennifer Tipton Cappoen, Chris Curry, Sarah Foreman, Theresa Lewis Goode, Clint Moore, Greg D. Rieves, Barry Slate, Donna K. Teal, Zane Williard, Tazmen Carlisle, Marsha Heim, Lynette Dickerson, Mark Rainey

www.themailbox.com

Manufactured in the United States
10 9 8 7 6 5 4 3 2 1

Table of Contents

Welcome!

This song may be simple, but it sure is catchy! After singing it a few times, your youngsters just might want to join in! So invite your class to sing along to the tune of "Shoo Fly."

Welcome to school today!
Welcome to school today!
Welcome to school today!
We have come to learn and play!

Eva Bareis, Cinnamon Hill Preschool
Rapid City, SD

Welcome To Our Class!

Begin the day with this toe-tapping tune, and students are sure to feel welcome in their new classroom!

(sung to the tune of "London Bridge")

Welcome, welcome to our class,
To our class, to our class.
Welcome, welcome to our class,
Hello, [child's name]!

Ada Goren, Winston-Salem, NC

What Did You Do in School?

Here's a simple song that will help your youngsters remember their first day in school. Invite students to name different activities from the day, such as playing, singing, and dancing. Then incorporate their answers in the song below. Now, when students' parents ask what they did in school, your youngsters can respond in song!

(sung to the tune of "Johnny Works With One Hammer")

Today I [played] with new friends,
New friends, new friends.
Today I [played] with new friends.
We had lots of fun!

Eva Bareis, Cinnamon Hill Preschool, Rapid City, SD

Welcome To Preschool

(sung to the tune of "Up on the Housetop")

We made some friends today, today.
We had lots of fun, I'd say.
Blocks, puzzles, and other games to play.
Welcome to preschool. Hooray! Hooray!

Mary Summers
Hobbitts Preschool
Richfield, OH

It's Cool to Go to School

With the corresponding hand motions, this song is perfect to perform for moms and dads on a special school visitation day or open house night!

(sung to the tune of "A Hunting We Will Go")

I'm learning every day.
I'm learning every day.
It's oh so cool to go to school!   *Give two*
I'm learning every day.   *thumbs-up.*

I'm learning about letters.
I'm learning about letters.
That's what I need so I can read!   *Pretend to open*
I'm learning about letters.   *and read a book.*

I'm learning about numbers.
I'm learning about numbers.
Without a doubt then I can count!   *Count on fingers.*
I'm learning about numbers.

I'm learning how to write.
I'm learning how to write.
Curves and lines suit me just fine!   *"Write" letters in air.*
I'm learning how to write.

I'm learning to make friends.
I'm learning to make friends.
I want to play with you today!   *Hug a friend.*
I'm learning to make friends.

Kathy Thurman
Southern Elementary
Somerset, KY

Fall 5

National Grandparents Day Song

Teach your little ones this song to sing to their grandfriends on National Grandparents Day.

(sung to the tune of "I'm a Little Teapot")

I'm a little grandchild, cute and sweet.
Somebody thinks that I'm pretty neat.
When I need a friend, just hear me shout,
"Hey, Grand[ma], can you come out?"

Child points to grandparent.

adapted from a song by Joe Montgomery
St. Mary of the Assumption School
Herman, PA

Grandfriends Are Special

Here's a simple song that you can use following a visit from one of your grandfriends. Won't the singing make him or her feel special?

(sung to the tune of "Jimmie Crack Corn")

My grandfriend is a special friend.
My grandfriend is a special friend.
My grandfriend is a special friend.
He/she [reads books] with me.

Planting Apple Seeds

Thanks to Johnny Appleseed, there are apples aplenty. Here's a song that invites your students to pretend to plant apple seeds row by row. Just include a different child's name every time you repeat the verse. Hurrah!

(sung to the tune of "The Ants Go Marching")

[Johnny] is planting apple seeds.
Hurrah, hurrah!
Yes, [Johnny] is planting apple seeds.
Hurrah, hurrah!
[He's] planting seeds so trees will grow.
[He's] planting seeds, row by row.
Say thank you now to [Johnny] Appleseed.
There are apples for you and me.

Linda Ludlow
Pittsboro, IN

Celebrate With a Song

Johnny Appleseed's birthday is such a special occasion, singing "Happy Birthday" is simply not enough! Teach your youngsters the following tune and celebrate with a song just for Johnny!

(sung to the tune of "Deck the Halls")

Let's all celebrate a birthday.
Happy birthday, Johnny Appleseed!
It's a very special birthday.
Happy birthday, Johnny Appleseed!

Another Apple Anthem

(sung to the tune of "Twinkle, Twinkle, Little Star")

Shiny, shiny, apple red,
Hanging high above my head.
On my tiptoes, reaching high.
One last stretch, it's worth a try.
Shiny, shiny, apple red,
Grabbed it, ate it, now I'm fed!

Jana Sanderson
Rainbow School
Stockton, CA

Apples up on Top

How can you pick apples that are high in a tree?
Sing this song to discover a clever solution!

(sung to the tune of "Up on the Housetop")

Up in the treetop, way up high.
Three red apples for my pie.
How will I get them to the ground?
I'll shake that tree 'til they fall down!
Shake, shake, shake!
Watch them fall!
Shake, shake, shake,
I'll catch them all!
Oh, into my basket,
One, two, three!
No more apples in the tree.

Eva Bareis, Cinnamon Hill Preschool
Rapid City, SD

A Wiggly Worm

This happy apple tune is perfect for a fall day! Add some action by using your index finger to represent the worm, popping him out of the apple (your fist) at the appropriate point in the song. Or, if desired, make an apple-and-worm puppet. Simply cut a large apple shape from laminated red construction paper. Cut a hole in the apple large enough to slide a hand through. Attach two small wiggle eye stickers to the toe of a green sock. When you're ready to perform the song, slip the sock onto one hand and hold the apple in the other. Make the worm appear at just the right moment!

(sung to the tune of "Boom, Boom, Ain't It Great to Be Crazy?")

Chorus
Yum! Yum! Don't you know I love apples?
Yum! Yum! Don't you know I love apples?
Red and green and yellow, too.
Yum! Yum! Don't you know I love apples?

Verse 1
Way up high in an apple tree, I saw two eyes look at me.
I reached for an apple; it started to squirm. Oops! I found a wiggly worm!

Chorus

Verse 2
That wiggly worm is a friend of mine. We eat apples all the time.
I let him crawl back to that tree. Hey! I see that worm looking at me!

Chorus

Sandy Moons
Parkcrest E.C.E., Long Beach, CA

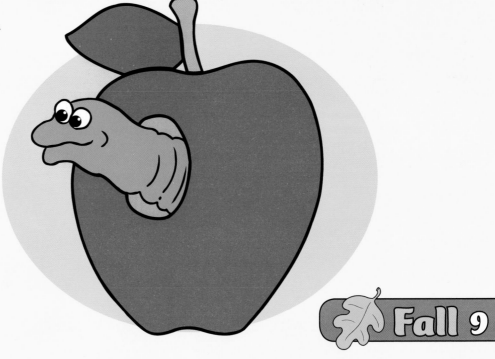

An Apple Surprise

Way up high in the apple tree,

A little brown worm smiled at me.

I winked my eye,

And what do you suppose?

A shiny red apple dropped on my nose!

Dayle Timmons

Crunchy Apples

Here's a healthful snacktime poem that's sure to get your class in the mood for apples! For additional verses of the poem, replace the word *red* with other apple colors.

Oh, I wish I had a shiny [red] apple.
That is what I'd truly like to eat.
For if I had a shiny [red] apple,
I would have a crunchy, munchy treat!

Daphne L. Rivera
Bob Sikes Elementary School
Crestview, FL

Apple, Apple, Apple!

Give any apple unit some crunch with this lively song!

(sung to the tune of "Dreidel Song")

I picked a little apple.
I picked it from a tree.
It was red and shiny,
And juicy as can be!
I picked it from a tree.
Oh, apple, apple, apple,
It sure tastes good to me!
CRUNCH!

Lori A. Cohen
Buffalo, NY

An Apple Just for Me

You can use this poem for choral reading/reciting or sing it adapted to the tune of "Twinkle, Twinkle, Little Star." Either way, youngsters will want to sing it over and over just to get to the surprise ending!

Apple, apple on the tree;
Nice and shiny, just for me.
Little wormy on the ground
Spied that apple big and round.
Inch by inch he climbed that tree,
And he ate that apple instead of me!

Adapted from an idea by
Heather Fox, Badin Elementary, Badin, NC
Sandra Fox, Reedy Creek Elementary, Charlotte, NC

Lines 1 & 2

Lines 3 & 4

Line 5

Line 6

I'm a Little Scarecrow

(sung to the tune of "I'm a Little Teapot")

I'm a little scarecrow
Stuffed with hay.
Here I stand in a field all day.
When I see the crows
I like to shout,
"Hey! You crows, you better get out!"

Abby Carney
Kid's Connection
S. Hamilton, MA

Kelly Williams, Jacksboro, TX

Mr. Scarecrow

(sung to the tune of "Twinkle, Twinkle, Little Star")

Mr. Scarecrow standing tall,
You just don't scare me at all.
Stuffed with straw from head to toe.
Quite a funny guy to know.
Mr. Scarecrow standing tall,
You just don't scare me at all!

Hold hand above head and look up.
Shake head "no."
Touch head; then touch toes.
Hold tummy and chuckle.
Hold hand above head and look up.
Shake head "no."

Betty Silkunas
Lansdale, PA

Tree Tune

Youngsters will have "tree-mendous" fun exercising while they sing this ode to trees! Just have students stand tall with their arms above their heads like branches. Lead them in shaking their hands when they sing "leaves," bending their arms up and down when they sing "branches," touching their waists when they sing "trunk," and touching and wiggling their toes when they sing "roots."

(sung to the tune of "Head and Shoulders")

Leaves, branches, trunk, and roots,
Trunk and roots.
Leaves, branches, trunk, and roots,
Trunk and roots.
Nuts and berries, seeds and fruit,
Leaves, branches, trunk, and roots,
Trunk and roots.

Diane Crandell
Chelsea Community Education Preschool
Chelsea, MI

Up on the Treetop

As your little ones sing this fall tune, have them pretend to crunch, crunch, crunch through the leaves.

(sung to the tune of "Up on the Housetop")

Up on the treetop
Watch the leaves.
They are changing.
You can see
Red and orange,
Yellow and brown.
Pretty soon they'll all fall down!

Crunch, crunch, crunch!
Walk through the leaves.
Crunch, crunch, crunch!
Walk through the leaves.
Up on the treetop
In the fall,
Leaves are changing.
Watch them all!

Laurel Jonas
Trinity Lutheran
Wisconsin Dells, WI

Autumn Is Here

Have each child tape die-cut leaves to a length of yarn or clear fishing line. Then invite him to whirl and swirl his leaves while singing this autumn song.

(sung to the tune of "Did You Ever See a Lassie?")

The leaves are really changing,
And changing, and changing.
The leaves are really changing,
For autumn is here.

See red leaves and brown leaves,
And green leaves and gold leaves.
The leaves are really changing,
For autumn is here!

Linda Rice Ludlow, Bethesda Christian School
Brownsburg, IN

Jumping Into Fall!

Students rake in the compliments when they perform this quick and fun fall poem!

In the fall, all the leaves fall down—
Orange, yellow, red, and brown.
I pile them up as neat as a pin.
Then I run
And jump right in!

Wiggle fingers down to the floor.

Make a gathering motion.
Run in place.
Jump up; then sit down.

Elizabeth Farella
Kiddie Junction
Levittown, NY

Leaves Come Falling Down

Cut a class supply of leaf shapes from red, orange, and brown paper. Then give each child one leaf to drop as its corresponding color is sung.

(sung to the tune of "Shoo Fly")

Red leaves,
Come falling down.
Orange leaves,
Come falling down.
Brown leaves,
Come falling down.
Show us autumn's come to town!

LeeAnn Collins, Sunshine Preschool, Lansing, MI

Tossing Leaves

Here's a lively song that little ones will fall for! If desired, scatter a supply of construction paper leaves on the floor and invite youngsters to toss the leaves as they sing. Hooray!

(sung to the tune of "The Ants Go Marching")

I like to toss the leaves up high.
Hooray! Hooray!
I like to toss the leaves up high.
Hooray! Hooray!
I toss them up
And they come down,
Yellow, orange, red, and brown!
Oh, I like to toss the leaves,
Toss the leaves
Way up high
In the sky!

Diana Shepard, First Presbyterian Preschool
Wilmington, NC

Busy Squirrel

If your little ones are feeling squirrelly this fall, keep them moving with the motions of this action poem. Or provide youngsters with acorns to "bury" under a table as you chant the first verse of the poem and then "dig up" when you recite the second verse.

 Gray squirrel, gray squirrel

 Doesn't make a sound,

 As he buries acorns
Underneath the ground.

 Later, when it's cold out

 And food cannot be found,

 The gray squirrel will dig
His acorns from the ground.

Linda Rice Ludlow, Bethesda Christian School,
Brownsburg, IN

Mr. Squirrel

Who's that scampering up the tree,

Carrying acorns...1, 2, 3?

It's Mr. Squirrel with a tail so furry.

He's ready for winter, so don't you worry!

Betty Silkunas, Lansdale, PA

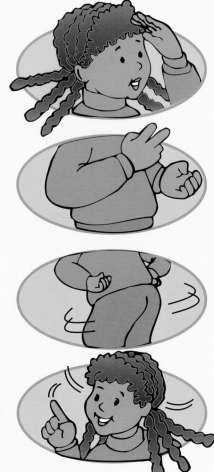

I'm a Firefighter

(sung to the tune of "I'm a Little Teapot")

I'm a firefighter.	*Point to self.*
Here's my hose.	*Outstretch arm with finger pointed.*
I put out fires	
As everyone knows.	
When I see a fire	*Hand over brow.*
I douse it out.	*Outstretch arm with finger pointed.*
"Thank you! Thank you!"	
People shout!	

Linda Rice Ludlow
Bethesda Christian School
Brownsburg, IN

Help Is on the Way!

Help youngsters remember 9-1-1 in an emergency with this useful song!

(sung to the tune of "Three Blind Mice")

9-1-1, 9-1-1—
Help's on the way; help's on the way.
When I need help, I know what to do.
I dial this number for me and for you.
It calls the police and the firehouse too.
It's 9-1-1.

Jessica Mathews
Footprints , Vernon, NJ

In Case of Fire...

Use this catchy tune to teach youngsters the three numbers to call if there is a fire. 9-1-1!

(sung to the tune of "Head and Shoulders")

When you see a fire, call 9-1-1!
When you see a fire, call 9-1-1!
9-1-1!
The fire truck will come!
When you see a fire, call 9-1-1!

Helpful Firefighters

(sung to the tune of "She'll Be Comin' Round the Mountain")

Oh, firefighters wear big rubber boots.	*Stomp feet two times.*
Oh, firefighters wear big rubber boots.	*Stomp feet two times.*
Oh, when fire causes trouble,	
They'll be right there on the double!	
Oh, firefighters wear big rubber boots.	*Stomp feet two times.*
Oh, firefighters drive a great big truck.	*Say, "Vroom! Vroom!"*
Oh, firefighters drive a great big truck.	*Say, "Vroom! Vroom!"*
Oh, when fire causes trouble,	
They'll be right there on the double!	
Oh, firefighters drive a great big truck.	*Say, "Vroom! Vroom!"*
Oh, firefighters spray a fire hose.	*Say, "Woosh! Woosh!"*
Oh, firefighters spray a fire hose.	*Say, "Woosh! Woosh!"*
Oh, when fire causes trouble,	
They'll be right there on the double!	
Oh, firefighters spray a fire hose.	*Say, "Woosh! Woosh!*
Oh, firefighters put the fire out.	*Say, "All done!"*
Oh, firefighters put the fire out.	*Say, "All done!"*
Oh, when fire causes trouble,	
They'll be right there on the double!	
Oh, firefighters put the fire out.	*Say, "All done!"*

Lucia Kemp Henry
Fallon, NV

Oh, No! A Fire!

Oh, no! There's a fire!

Bring hoses, ladders, axes, too.

Firefighters to the rescue!

Wear boots, hats,

safety masks;

Spray the water, what a task!

Saving people night and day,

Thanks, firefighters! Hip hip hooray!

Carrie Lacher, Friday Harbor, WA

Columbus Day March

Left, right, left, right! Your youngsters will enjoy marching to the beat while singing this catchy verse about Christopher Columbus. For added fun, start out singing the song slowly and then pick up speed with each repetition.

(sung to the tune of "The Ants Go Marching")

Columbus sailed the ocean blue—hurrah, hurrah!

He sailed in 1492—hurrah, hurrah!

Columbus sailed the ocean blue.

He sailed in 1492.

He had hoped to reach the east, sailing west.

Oh, he tried his best,

On his quest!

adapted from an idea by
June M. Ray
Henry A. Malley Memorial Library
Broadus, MT

Five Spotted Owls

"Whooo" will enjoy this counting rhyme? Youngsters, that's who! Make five brown construction paper owl cutouts. Prepare each cutout for flannelboard use. Arrange the owls in a row on your flannelboard. Then perform the chant with your class, removing each owl when indicated.

Five spotted owls on a Saturday night,
Perched in a tree in the full moonlight.
The fifth spotted owl said, "It's time to eat!"
And she went looking for a late night treat.

Hold up five fingers.
Make a circle with arms above head.
Rub tummy.
Look from side to side.

Four spotted owls on a Saturday night,
Perched in a tree in the full moonlight.
The fourth spotted owl said, "It's time to fly!"
And he flapped his wings and said, "Goodbye."

Hold up four fingers.
Make a circle with arms above head.
Flap arms.
Wave goodbye.

Three spotted owls on a Saturday night,
Perched in a tree in the full moonlight.
The third spotted owl said, "No time to rest!"
And she flew away to build a nest.

Hold up three fingers.
Make a circle with arms above head.
Shake finger.
Pantomime gathering sticks.

Two spotted owls on a Saturday night,
Perched in a tree in the full moonlight.
The second spotted owl said, "I just can't stay.
I've got to go! It's time to play!"

Hold up two fingers.
Make a circle with arms above head.
Point to self.
Wiggle body.

One spotted owl on a Saturday night,
Perched in a tree in the full moonlight.
This spotted owl said, "Hoo, hoo, hoo!
I can't think of anything left to do!"

Hold up one finger.
Make a circle with arms above head.
Cup hands around mouth.
Throw arms out to the sides.

Elizabeth Schneller
Kehoe France School, Metairie, LA

Nighttime Noises

Who's poking around outside when night falls? Bats and owls and raccoons—that's who! As you sing this lively tune, invite youngsters to add the sound effects to each verse.

(sung to the tune of "This Little Light Of Mine")

I hear a noise outside.
It's a flapping bat. Whoosh!
I hear a noise outside.
It's a flapping bat. Whoosh!
What's it doin' outside?
It's chasing a bug.
Hear it flap, hear it flap, hear it flap!

I hear a noise outside.
It's an old hoot owl. Hoot!
I hear a noise outside.
It's an old hoot owl. Hoot!
What's it doin' outside?
It's chasing a mouse.
Hear it hoot, hear it hoot, hear it hoot!

I hear a noise outside.
It's an old raccoon. Splash!
I hear a noise outside.
It's an old raccoon. Splash!
What's it doin' outside?
It's chasing a fish.
Hear it splash, hear it splash, hear it splash!

adapted from an idea by Linda Blassingame
JUST 4 & 5 Developmental Laboratory, Mobile, AL

Found a Pumpkin

If you're planning a trip to the pumpkin patch this fall, sing this simple song after students pick their pumpkins!

(sung to the tune of "Found a Peanut")

Found a pumpkin,
Found a pumpkin,
Found a pumpkin today.
Today I found a pumpkin.
Found a pumpkin today.

If desired, sing additional verses, re-placing *found a pumpkin* with *cut it open, scooped the seeds out,* and *carved a face.*

Bonnie Elizabeth Vontz
Cheshire Country Day School
Milldale, CT

Pick a Pumpkin

It's pumpkin-pickin' time! Get your youngsters in the mood by singing this little ditty!

(sung to the tune of "London Bridge")

Pick a pumpkin from the vine,
Pumpkin round, pumpkin fine.
Pick a pumpkin from the vine.
Let's pick pumpkins!

Pick a pumpkin from the vine.
You pick yours; I'll pick mine.
Pick a pumpkin from the vine.
Let's pick pumpkins!

Betty Silkunas
Lower Gwynedd Elementary
Ambler, PA

From Seed to Pie!

Use this lively song to introduce little ones to the life cycle of a pumpkin! Sing the song five more times, each time replacing the first, second, and fourth lines with the next song line in the provided sequence.

(sung to the tune of "The Farmer in the Dell")

The seed is in the ground.
The seed is in the ground.
Hi-ho, the pumpkin patch!
The seed is in the ground.

Continue with these lines:
The seed grows a sprout.
The sprout grows a vine.
The vine grows a bloom.
The bloom grows a pumpkin.
We make a pumpkin pie.

Diane Donovan, Cheryl Ann Preschool, Celina, OH

Pumpkin on the Vine

This is a pleasing pumpkin song!

(sung to the tune of "The Farmer in the Dell")

The pumpkin on the vine,
The pumpkin on the vine—
I picked the one that weighs a ton,
And that's the one that's mine!

I made two scary eyes
And a mouth that's oversized.
My mother took the other goop
And made some pumpkin pies.

The pumpkin on the vine,
The pumpkin on the vine
Is now a jack-o'-lantern,
And you should see it shine!

Sally Starr
Twin Beach Elementary
West Bloomfield, MI

A Cornucopia Chorus

Harvest a classroom of happy youngsters with this fruit and vegetable medley!

(sung to the tune of "Clementine")

[There's a pumpkin], [there's a pumpkin]
In the cornucopia!
[There's a pumpkin], [there's a pumpkin]
In the cornucopia!

Sing additional verses, replacing the underlined phrase with phrases such as *there's an apple, there is corn, there's a squash,* and *there are grapes.*

Angie Kutzer, Garrett Elementary, Mebane, NC

It's October!

Apples, pumpkins, and trick-or-treating—there's nothing like October! Teach your little ones this song. Then discuss other fun things about October and make up more verses. Yee-ha!

(sung to the tune of "She'll Be Comin' Round the Mountain")

It's October and it's time to have some fun. Yee-ha!
It's October and it's time to have some fun. Yee-ha!
Pickin' apples up so high
For a fresh-baked apple pie.
It's October and it's time to have some fun. Yee-ha!

Oh, it's time to head out to the pumpkin patch. Yee-ha!
Yes, it's time to head out to the pumpkin patch. Yee-ha!
To the patch to choose a pumpkin,
Dressed up like a country bumpkin.
Oh, it's time to head out to the pumpkin patch. Yee-ha!

We will all go trick-or-treatin' Halloween. Yee-ha!
We will all go trick-or-treatin' Halloween. Yee-ha!
Saying "Boo!" to those we meet,
Getting lots of things to eat.
We will all go trick-or-treatin' Halloween. Yee-ha!

adapted from an idea by Kelly Williams
Jacksboro, TX

A Penny for Your Pumpkin

This fingerplay reinforces counting skills and coin recognition as well! To make this poem worth a lot of learning and fun, put five to ten felt pumpkin shapes on a flannelboard; then give each of the same number of children a coin cutout. In turn, invite each child to show his coin cutout. Identify the coin cutout (penny, nickel, dime, quarter); then have him exchange it for a pumpkin as the class recites the rhyme.

[Five] orange pumpkins in a pumpkin patch.
You know, the kind that are big and round and fat!
Along came a child with a [penny] to pay,
He bought a pumpkin and took it away.

Sherry Hammons, Tunica Elementary, Tunica, LA

Round Little Pumpkin

Here's a little tune, ripe for the picking!

(sung to the tune of "Five Little Ducks")

Round little pumpkin on the vine,
You look so orange.
You look so fine.
I think you're the one that I've plans for.
You will be the jack-o'-lantern by my door!

LeeAnn Collins
Sunshine House Preschool
Lansing, MI

Orange Pumpkin

Encourage youngsters to echo you as you sing this simple song. Once they are familiar with the song, divide the group in half and have them take turns echoing each other. Each time you repeat the song, substitute a different word to describe the jack-o'-lantern, such as *smiling, winking,* or *toothy.*

(sung to the tune of "Are You Sleeping?")

Orange pumpkin,
Orange pumpkin,
Soon you'll be,
Soon you'll be,
A [glowing] jack-o'-lantern,
A [glowing] jack-o'-lantern,
Just for me!
Just for me!

LeeAnn Collins

The Pumpkin in the Patch

Teach little ones this version of "The Farmer in the Dell" and have youngsters act it out accordingly.

The pumpkin's in the patch.
The pumpkin's in the patch.
Boo! Boo! It's Halloween.
The pumpkin's in the patch.

The pumpkin takes the cat…

The cat takes the bat…

The bat takes the ghost…

The ghost takes the treats…

We all say, "Trick or treat"…

Pumpkin and Shakin'

Shake up some fall fun with these nifty milk-carton shakers. To make one, paint an empty half-pint milk carton orange. When the paint is dry, place a handful of dried beans inside the carton. Cut several lengths of green curling ribbon; then tape one end of each length inside the carton top. Curl the lengths of ribbon to resemble vines. Staple two construction-paper leaves to the top of the carton while stapling the top shut. If desired, glue black construction-paper features on one side of the carton to create a jack-o'-lantern face. Now get your youngsters shaking as they sing their Halloween favorites or the song below!

(sung to the tune of "Baby Bumblebee")

I'm picking out a pumpkin on a vine.
I want one big and fat and fine.
I'm picking out a pumpkin on a vine,
Oh, I see mine!

I'm pulling on a pumpkin on a vine.
It's so big and fat and fine!
I'm pulling on a pumpkin on a vine.
Snap! It's mine!

craft idea by Nancy K. Mazur, St. Joseph Preschool
Wapakoneta, OH

Halloween Dress-Up

Invite your little ones to tell you about their Halloween costumes. After they share their disguises, teach them this tune, substituting the costumes your children have named.

(sung to the tune of "Twinkle, Twinkle, Little Star")

I'm dressed up for Halloween—
Best little [cat] you've ever seen!
Here I am in my disguise.
I have changed before your eyes.
I'm dressed up for Halloween—
Best little [cat] you've ever seen.

Lucia Kemp Henry
Fallon, NV

What Costume Will You Wear?

Trick or treat! What will each of your little darlings pretend to be for Halloween?

(sung to the tune of "The Farmer in the Dell")

What costume will you wear?
What costume will you wear?
To trick-or-treat on Halloween,
What costume will you wear?

I will be a [princess].
I will be a [princess].
To trick-or-treat on Halloween,
I will be a [princess].

Christa J. Koch
Circle of Friends
Bethlehem, PA

Halloween Pretending

Each time you sing this song, invite a student to pretend to be the character of her choice. Pretending is fun!

(sung to the tune of "Clementine")

Halloween is such a fun time.
It's not scary, not for me.
I pretend I'm someone different.
It's as fun as fun can be.

Mary Sutula, Orlando, FL

Watch Out!

It's that time of year—ghosts and ghouls are lurking and searching for that big scare. Teach your little goblins this song and the accompanying motions. It's sure to turn those "ghasps" into "ghrins"!

(sung to the tune of "Santa Claus Is Comin' to Town")

You'd better watch out! You'd better beware!
You'd better believe you're in for a scare!
Halloween is coming tonight!

Point and shake finger.
Shiver.
Look wide-eyed.

Pumpkins aglow with snaggletoothed grins.
Skeletons jump right out of their skins.
Halloween is coming tonight!

Point to teeth.
Jump with arms out.
Look wide-eyed.

Spooky, cackling witches are stirring up their brew.
Mean-faced, green-faced Frankensteins are coming
　　after you!
　　　　BOO!

Stir with fists.
Walk stiff-legged.
Throw up hands.

Repeat first stanza to end the song.

Diane ZuHone Shore, Marietta, GA

An Unexpected Sight

Even monsters get scared sometimes! Encourage your children to be—that is, pretend to be—monsters. Then ask a volunteer to step away from the group. At the end of the poem, have that boy or girl skip back in sight just in time to scare the monsters.

Five little monsters
Haunting in the night.
The first one said,
"I'm not feeling just right."

The second one said,
"My skin is feeling wet."

The third one quivered,
"We're just scared, I bet."

The fourth one said,
"I can feel my heart pound."

The fifth one said,
"Shh! What was that sound?"

Then "Oooh" went the wind,
And on came the lights
As a wee little [girl/boy]
Came skipping into sight!

Lisa Cowman, Norwalk, OH

Thanksgiving Colors

Are you ready for the meal of the year? Here's a poem that builds excitement and reviews color words as well. Use the poem's pattern as a springboard for creating additional verses with other typical (or not so typical) Thanksgiving dishes. Gobble, gobble!

Orange is the pumpkin.
Yellow is the corn.
Brown is the turkey,
With stuffing to adorn.

Red are the cranberries.
Green are the beans.
Five delicious colors—
In a feast of my dreams.

Happy Thanksgiving!

adapted from an idea by
Jeanene Engelhardt
Workman Avenue School
Covina, CA

sun

moon

family

friends

Singing and Signing Thanks

Teach your little ones a new way to say "Thank you" using the hand sign as shown. Then sign thank you—along with the additional hand signs shown, if desired—as you sing the following song.

(sung to the tune of "Twinkle, Twinkle, Little Star")

Thank you for the sun so bright.
Thank you for the moon at night.
Thank you for my family.
Thanks for friends who play with me.
Thanks for everything I see.
I am thankful, yes sirree!

Turkey Talk

Get geared up for the holidays by inviting youngsters to act out the following turkey poem. Gobble, gobble, gobble!

Mr. Turkey struts all around,
Pecking at the corn
Scattered on the ground.
See him walk with a wobble, wobble, wobble.
Hear him talk with a gobble, gobble, gobble.

Lajeanne Ashley
Helena Elementary School
Timberlake, NC

Where's That Turkey?

Here's a quick song to celebrate that famous gobbler. Encourage students to waddle to the rhythm as you sing the song together.

(sung to the tune of "I'm a Little Teapot")

I'm a little turkey,
Waddling through town.
Here are my feathers: orange, red, and brown.
I will run and hide if I hear you say,
"It will soon be Thanksgiving Day!"

Bonnie Elizabeth Vontz
Cheshire Country Day School
Milldale, CT

Did You Ever See a Turkey?

Reinforce color recognition with this turkey tune. In advance, cut out a class supply of red, brown, yellow, and orange construction paper feathers. Give each child one feather. As the class sings the song below, have each student hold up his feather when its color is mentioned.

(sung to the tune of "Did You Ever See a Lassie?")

Did you ever see a turkey, a turkey, a turkey
As he struts around the farmyard with feathers so bright?
With red ones and brown ones and yellow
   ones and orange ones,
Did you ever see a turkey with feathers so bright?

Cele McCloskey and Brenda Peters, Dallastown, PA

Wingo

Put a turkey twist on a traditional spelling song for some fine-feathered fun! Print the letters *W, I, N, G,* and *O* on separate cards and have students hold them up. Substitute a wing flap motion as you drop each letter of Wingo's name from subsequent verses.

(sung to the tune of "Bingo")

There was a farmer who had a turkey,
And Wingo was his name-o!
W-I-N-G-O, W-I-N-G-O, W-I-N-G-O,
And Wingo was his name-o!

Karla Parker, Southern Elementary, Somerset, KY

Here Turkey, Turkey

(sung to the tune of "Dreidel Song")

I saw a little turkey
Standing by a tree.
It gobbled and it wobbled,
Then ran away from me!

Oh, turkey, turkey, turkey,
Please come out and play!
I promise not to eat you
On Thanksgiving Day!

Turkey in the Farmyard

(sung to the tune of "Kookaburra")

Turkey in the farmyard,
Strut happily.
Show all your feathers,
Bright as can be.
Gobble, gobble, turkey.
Gobble, gobble, turkey.
Such a sight to see!

Hold up open hand.
Wave hand.
Wiggle fingers.

Wiggle thumb.

Wave hand.

LeeAnn Collins
Sunshine House Preschool
Lansing, MI

Gobble, Gobble!

(sung to the tune of "If You're Happy and You Know It")

Mr. Turkey struts around, struts around.
Mr. Turkey struts around, struts around.
Mr. Turkey struts around,
Eating grain off the ground.
Mr. Turkey struts around, struts around.

Make wings with arms and strut around.

Mr. Turkey's big and round, big and round.
Mr. Turkey's big and round, big and round.
Mr. Turkey's big and round,
He's the biggest that we've found.
Mr. Turkey's big and round, big and round.

Hold arms out to show fat tummy.

"Gobble, gobble!" says the turkey; that's his sound.
"Gobble, gobble!" says the turkey; that's his sound.
"Gobble, gobble!" is his sound,
He gobble-gobbles 'til he's found.
"Gobble, gobble!" says the turkey; that's his sound.

Gobble like a turkey!

Now Thanksgiving Day is here, day is here.
Now Thanksgiving Day is here, day is here.
Now Thanksgiving Day is here,
Mr. Turkey needs to fear.
Now Thanksgiving Day is here, day is here.

Make a scared face with a hand on each cheek.

Eat more veggies!

Let's Eat!

Mouths will be watering when you sing this appetizing Thanksgiving song. Pass the stuffing, please!

(sung to the tune of "Are You Sleeping?")

Turkey dinner, turkey dinner,
Gather 'round. Gather 'round.
Who will get the drumstick,
Yummy, yummy drumstick?
Let's sit down. Let's sit down.

Cornbread muffin, chestnut stuffin',
Pudding pie, one foot high!
All of us were thinner,
'Til we came to dinner,
Me-oh-my! Me-oh-my!

Lajeanne Ashley
Timberlake, NC

A Healthful Feast

Children from various cultural backgrounds will enjoy naming favorite foods in order to cook up new verses for this tasty song. Continue until each child has had a turn and all tummies are full!

(sung to the tune of "Pawpaw Patch")

Chorus:
Let's start cooking Thanksgiving dinner.
Let's start cooking Thanksgiving dinner.
Let's start cooking Thanksgiving dinner.
My, oh my, what a healthful feast!

Cook the [turkey]; put it on the table.
Cook the [turkey]; put it on the table.
Cook the [turkey]; put it on the table.
My, oh my, what a healthful feast!

Winter

Winter

W is for winter, a cold time of year.
Wrap arms around torso and shiver.

I is for ice-skating far and near.
Pretend to skate.

N is for nighttime, all snowy and bright.
Lay head on "pillow" hands.

T is for trees with no leaves in sight.
Stretch arms up like tree branches.

E is for ears, so cold and red.
Cup hands around ears.

R is for ready to ride on my sled!
Jump up and down with excitement.

I Like Winter!

(sung to the tune of "London Bridge")

Wintertime is [frosty cold],
Frosty cold, frosty cold.
Wintertime is [frosty cold].
I like winter!

Sing additional verses, replacing the
underlined phrase with *stormy bold, snowy
white,* and *chilly bright.*

Lucia Kemp Henry
Fallon, NV

Light the Candles!

Brighten a celebration of Hanukkah (or Kwanzaa) with this luminous counting song! Start with the provided verse and then sing additional verses, increasing the candle count by one for each successive day of celebration. Brilliant!

(sung to the tune of "Found a Peanut")

Light [one candle], light [one candle];
"Happy Hanukkah!" we say.
It is day [one], it is day [one]
Of this joyful holiday!

LeeAnn Collins
Sunshine House Preschool
Lansing, MI

Twinkle, Twinkle

'Tis the season for holiday lights! Kwanzaa kinaras, Hanukkah menorahs, and Christmas tree lights are all around! Use the following song as you teach youngsters about any of these well-lit holidays.

(sung to the tune of "Twinkle, Twinkle, Little Star")

Twinkle, twinkle, candlelight,
Shining on this holiday night.
Shining bright for us to see
Just how special this time can be.
Twinkle, twinkle, candlelight,
Shining on this holiday night.

LeeAnn Collins

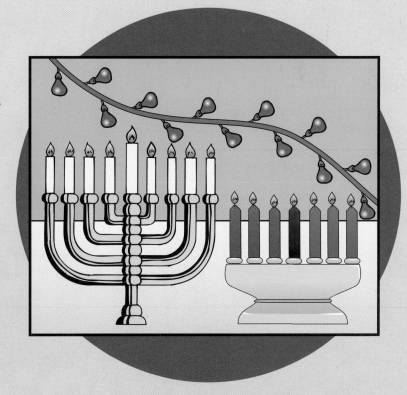

Ten Little Latkes

(sung to the tune of "Pawpaw Patch")

One little, two little, three little latkes;
Four little, five little, six little latkes;
Seven little, eight little, nine little latkes;
Ten little latkes for a Hanukkah treat!

We peeled and chopped and grated our potatoes.
Peeled and chopped and grated our potatoes.
We peeled and chopped and grated our potatoes.
Ten little latkes for a Hanukkah treat!

We put them in the pan and fried them in the oil.
Put them in the pan and fried them in the oil.
We put them in the pan and fried them in the oil.
Ten little latkes for a Hanukkah treat!

They fried and sizzled until they were brown.
Fried and sizzled until they were brown.
They fried and sizzled until they were brown.
Ten little latkes for a Hanukkah treat!

We smelled them, ate them—mmm…how delicious!
Smelled them, ate them—mmm…how delicious!
We smelled them, ate them—mmm…how delicious!
No more latkes for a Hanukkah treat!

Kathy Cotton
Stepping Stones Preschool, Westport, CT

Five Little Latkes

Who ate all the Hanukkah latkes? Have students perform the following fingerplay to find out!

Five little latkes, not one more.   *Hold up five fingers.*
Mother ate one and then there were four.   *Hold up four fingers.*
Four little latkes waiting for me.
Father ate one and then there were three. *Hold up three fingers.*
Three little latkes ready to chew.
Brother ate one and then there were two.   *Hold up two fingers.*
Two little latkes, oh what fun!
Sister ate a latke and then there was one. *Hold up one finger.*
One little latke, the tastiest one.
I ate it all up and then there were none. *Hold fingers in the shape of a zero.*

Betty Silkunas
Lower Gwynedd Elementary
Ambler, PA.

Christmas Celebrations

Gather your little carolers to sing about familiar Christmas traditions! Sing this song several times, spotlighting a different tradition during each rendition. (See suggestions below.)

(sung to the tune of "For He's a Jolly Good Fellow")

People celebrate Christmas,
People celebrate Christmas,
People celebrate Christmas
By [putting up a tree].

By [putting up a tree],
By [putting up a tree],
People celebrate Christmas
By [putting up a tree].

Other suggestions: *wrapping up some gifts, hanging up a wreath, jingling jingle bells, baking Christmas treats*

Suzanne Moore
Irving, TX

Ring-a-ling-a-ling

If it's Christmas and you know it, sing this song!

(sung to the tune of "If You're Happy and You Know It")

If it's Christmas and you know it, [ring a bell]!
If it's Christmas and you know it, [ring a bell]!
If it's Christmas and you know it,
Then your face will surely show it!
If it's Christmas and you know it, [ring a bell]!

Sing additional verses, replacing the underlined phrase with *trim a tree, wrap a gift,* and *say ,"Ho! Ho! Ho!"* in turn.

Ada Goren
Winston-Salem, NC

Santa Had a Christmas Tree

Add to the fun of this tune by preparing a few props. Gather the following items: a paper star covered with glitter, a large jingle bell, a paper Christmas bulb and a box wrapped in holiday paper. (Put a couple of blocks in the box, so it will rattle when shaken.) Ask four student volunteers to hold the items in front of the group as you sing. As each item is mentioned in the song, have the designated child hold it up or shake it to make a noise.

(sung to the tune of "Old MacDonald Had a Farm")

Santa had a Christmas tree,
Ho, ho, ho, ho, ho!
And on that tree he had a star,
Ho, ho, ho, ho, ho!
With a twinkle, twinkle here
And a twinkle, twinkle there.
Here a twinkle, there a twinkle,
Everywhere a twinkle, twinkle!
Santa had a Christmas tree,
Ho, ho, ho, ho, ho!

Continue with additional verses:

And on that tree he had a bell…With a jingle, jingle here…
And on that tree he had a light…With a sparkle, sparkle here…
And under that tree he had a gift…With a rattle, rattle here…

Diana Shepard, First Presbyterian Preschool, Wilmington, NC

We Are Christmas Lights

What would Christmas lights say if they could talk?
They'd sing this happy song!

(sung to the tune of "Jingle Bells")

Verse:
We are Christmas lights,
And you know it's true—
We blink red and green
And sometimes white and blue!
We decorate your tree
To make your spirits bright.
Just look at all our colors
When we sparkle every night!

Chorus:
We blink red; we blink green;
We blink white and blue!
Yes, we blink at Christmastime; we do it just for you!
Oh, we blink red; we blink green;
We blink white and blue!
Have a Merry Christmas and a Happy New Year too!

Jane Hosford
Crossgates Methodist Children's Center
Brandon, MS

S-A-N-T-A!

As youngsters eagerly await the arrival of Santa Claus, have them sing this seasonal adaptation of "Bingo." For added holiday excitement, provide each of several children with a bell. Sing the song a second time and direct students to shake the bells instead of singing the *S*. Continue singing the song and jingling the bells until all of the letters have been eliminated. Ho, ho, ho!

There was a man with a long white beard,
And Santa was his name-o!
S-A-N-T-A! S-A-N-T-A! S-A-N-T-A!
And Santa was his name-o!

Cathy Schmidt
De Pere Co-op Nursery School
Green Bay, WI

Counting Cookies

Your little ones are sure to enjoy this sweet cookie countdown. With each consecutive verse another cookie disappears! To extend the learning opportunities, create flannelboard cookie pieces and a reindeer sock puppet for students to use as they recite the poem.

[Five] little cookies sitting on a plate,
Waiting for Santa.
He was running late!
Along came a reindeer,
Guess what he ate…
Crunch!

[Four] little cookies sitting on a plate,…

Merrilee Walker
Richmond, RI

Five Senses of the Seasons

Use a scented, tasty gingerbread man to explore the five senses with your youngsters. Teach them the following poem. Then extend the poem by making a class book shaped like a gingerbread man. Program each page of the book with a different sense. Then have youngsters look through magazines, catalogs, and advertising circulars to find holiday items to cut and glue on each page. Then, for a fun follow-up, make and eat gingerbread cookies.

Oh, Gingerbread Man, can you see
The shiny lights on the Christmas tree?

Oh, Gingerbread Man, can you hear
Silvery sleigh bells ringing near?

Oh, Gingerbread Man, can you sniff
Goodies that are baking? Take a whiff!

Oh, Gingerbread Man, can you feel
Santa's beard? Is it real?

Oh, Gingerbread Man, can you taste
The candies decorating your waist?

Oh, Gingerbread Man, your senses are so fine.
Will you help me work on mine? Yum!

adapted from a poem by Theresa Moonitz
Dr. Ronald McNair School P.S. 147 Q
Cambria Heights, NY

Hear

paper ripping–Rebecca

carols–Charles

"Ho! ho! ho!"–Mickayla

cash registers–Cassie

pots and pans–Trey

mixer–Blake

singing–Georgie

chain saw–Brandon

Holiday Senses

Use this cute poem to revisit the five senses and then extend the poem into a brainstorming activity. Write each of the five senses on a separate sheet of chart paper. Then list other holiday-related activities children name under the correct sensory headings. It's beginning to look, feel, taste, smell, and sound like Christmas!

At holiday time, it's nice to see
A lovely decorated Christmas tree.

At holiday time, it's nice to hear
Jingle bells ring on flying reindeer.

At holiday time, it's nice to feel
Santa's beard. Is it real?

At holiday time, it's nice to lick
A red and white striped candy stick.

At holiday time, it's fun to smell
Gingerbread cookies with sweet frosting gel.

Isn't it great? Isn't it fine
To use the five senses at holiday time?

Theresa Moonitz
Dr. Ronald McNair School P.S. 147 Q
Cambria Heights, NY

Candy Cane Chorus

There won't be a dry mouth in the bunch as youngsters sing this ode to a favorite sweet minty treat!

(sung to the tune of "O Christmas Tree")

O candy cane, O candy cane,
You're minty and delightful!
O candy cane, O candy cane,
I love you, every biteful.
Your tasty flavor is so sweet.
Your handle makes you fun to eat.
O candy cane, O candy cane,
I love your stripes and flavor!

Ten Little Reindeer

This reindeer romp keeps all ten little fingers busy until they end up on top of each child's head as antlers!

One little reindeer, nose all aglow.
Two little reindeer, standing in the snow.
Three little reindeer, looking all around.
Four little reindeer, stomping on the ground.
Five little reindeer, all on Christmas Eve.
Six little reindeer, ready to take leave.
Seven little reindeer, hear the bells a-jingle.
Eight little reindeer, ready for Kris Kringle.
Nine little reindeer, hitched up to the sleigh.
Ten little reindeer bringing gifts on Christmas Day!

Joy Hollabaugh, Lake Trafford Elementary, Imokalee, FL

Rudolph to the Rescue!

All the reindeer are here.
They are ready to go!
But how can they see
Out in the snow?

Put hands to head for antlers.
Prance in place.

Shrug shoulders.

They need a little light
To show them the way.
Here comes Rudolph!
Hip, hip, hooray!

Hand to brow, eyes straining to see.

Point finger.
Throw up hands and cheer.

Barb Stefaniuk
Kerrobert Tiny Tots Playschool
Kerrobert, Saskatchewan, Canada

Reindeer, Reindeer

Encourage youngsters to play the part of Rudolph as they join in this action chant. Give each child a red sticky dot to place on the tip of his nose. Ready, reindeer? It goes like this...

(chanted to the rhythm of "Teddy Bear, Teddy Bear")

Reindeer, reindeer, turn around.
Reindeer, reindeer, touch the ground.
Reindeer, reindeer, prance, prance, prance.
Reindeer, reindeer, do a little dance.
Reindeer, reindeer, line up for flight.
Reindeer, reindeer, say, "Good night!"

Karen Momrik
Elmira Elementary
Elmira, MI

The Rudolph Prance

Welcome Santa's season with some singing and dancing—or, actually, prancing! Give each child a red sticky dot to wear on her nose as she imitates Rudolph in this song.

(sung to the tune of "The Hokey-Pokey")

You put your [hooves] in; you put your [hooves] out.
You put your [hooves] in and you shake 'em all around!
You do the Rudolph Prance and you shake it all around—
That's what the reindeer do...wooooo!

Repeat the verse, substituting *antlers, red nose,* and *white tail* for the underlined word.

Florence Paola
Jane Ryan Elementary, Trumbull, CT

Call Rudolph!

Eight little reindeer pulling Santa's sled;

One fell down and bumped his head.

The elves called Santa and Santa said,

"Can seven little reindeer pull my sled?"

Seven little reindeer...
Six little reindeer...
Five little reindeer...
Four little reindeer...
Three little reindeer...
Two little reindeer...

One little reindeer pulling Santa's sled;
He fell down and bumped his head.
The elves called Santa and Santa said,
"Call Rudolph!"

Dayle Timmons
Alimancani Elementary School
Jacksonville, FL

Kwanzaa Candles

(sung to the tune of "Ten Little Indians")

One little, two little, three little candles,
Four little, five little, six little candles.
Seven little candles shine for Kwanzaa,
Shining and glowing in the night!

Red little, green little, black little candles.
Nice little, bright little Kwanzaa candles.
Shine, little candles, shine for Kwanzaa.
Oh, what a beautiful sight!

Lucia Kemp Henry
Fallon, NV

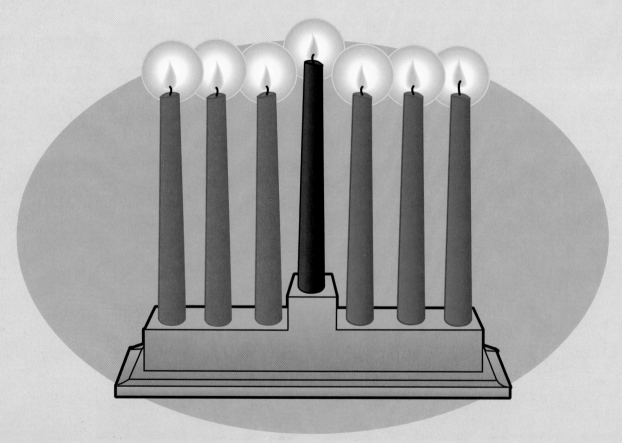

Kwanzaa Candles

Use this poem as a fingerplay or to introduce a real *kinara* (candleholder) and the *mishumaa saba* (seven candles) used during Kwanzaa.

Seven little candles all in a line,
Waiting to be lighted at Kwanzaa time.
Come let's count them—one, two, three,
Four, five, six, seven candles I see!

Christina Yuhouse
New Horizons School
Latrobe, PA

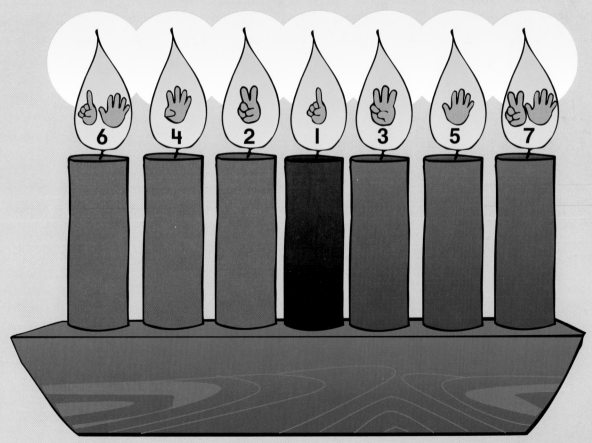

Moving Into a New Year

Gather your youngsters into a group circle; then get ready to stomp, hop, wiggle, and jump into the New Year!

(sung to the tune of "We Wish You a Merry Christmas")

We wish you a happy New Year,
We wish you a happy New Year,
We wish you a happy New Year,
Full of fun and good cheer!

Oh, come do a little stomping,
Oh, come do a little stomping,
Oh, come do a little stomping,
This happy New Year!

Oh, come do a little hopping....

Oh, come do a little wiggling....

Oh, come do a little jumping....

Dayle Timmons
Alimancani Elementary School
Jacksonville, FL

Happy New Year!

Get ready to ring in a new year with this lively tune. Are you ready? 10...9...8...

(sung to the tune of "Head, Shoulders, Knees, and Toes")

There's a new year on the way,
On the way!
There's a new year on the way,
On the way!
Let's celebrate the year and give a cheer! *(Say, "Hooray!")*
There's a new year on the way,
On the way!

It's Freezing, It's Snowing

What happens after a long, cold night of snow? You wake up to a world all aglow!

(sung to the tune of "A Tisket, a Tasket")

It's freezing. It's snowing.
The old wind is blowing.
I went to bed, laid down my head,
All the time not knowing,
Not knowing, not knowing,
The wind and snow kept going.
I woke up from a dark cold night
To see the world a-glowing!

Rebecca Fisch, Yeshiva Rabbi Hirsch, Brooklyn, NY

Good Hot Soup!

Serve up thoughts of warm, savory soup with this little ditty. After all, January is National Soup Month!

(sung to the tune of "Are You Sleeping?")

Good hot soup! Good hot soup!
Chicken rice tastes so nice.
Try chunky potato or vegetable tomato
In a cup; slurp it up!

LeeAnn Collins
Sunshine House Preschool
Lansing, MI

Winter Cold!

This little rhyme is a fun and gentle reminder for youngsters to bundle up during chilly weather!

Sniffling, sneezing, scratchy throat,
I went outside without my coat!

I had no hat upon my head,
And now I have to lie in bed!

Feverish, achy, stuffed-up nose,
I should have worn my winter clothes.

The next time I play in the snow,
I'll bundle up before I go!

Amie Johnson
Romeoville, IL

Winter Warm-Up

Singing this action song won't chase away winter; however, it will remind youngsters to bundle up when they head outdoors!

(sung to the tune of "Head and Shoulders")

Boots and mittens, scarf and hat, scarf and hat.
Pretend to put on clothing items.

Boots and mittens, scarf and hat, scarf and hat.
Pretend to put on clothing items.

I'm not cold when I put on all of that!
Shake head no.

Boots and mittens, scarf and hat, scarf and hat.
Pretend to put on clothing items.

Lesli Sutherland
W. C. Taylor Elementary, Trenton, MI

Put On Your Snow Clothes!

Invite your youngsters to dramatize bundling up with this wintry action poem.

Outside there's snow! The cold winds blow!
Let's bundle up and go, go, go!

Put on socks and long johns too.
The cold out there won't bother you.

Put on pants and a nice warm shirt.
Now that icy wind won't hurt!

Put on mittens and a hat.
You'll be comfy dressed like that!

Put on your boots. Your gear's complete!
You'll be warm down to your feet!

Outside there's snow! The cold winds blow!
We're bundled up! Let's go, go, go!

Look at the Snowflakes

(sung to the tune of "Up on the Housetop")

Look at the snowflakes swirl around.
Look how they fall to the ground.
Soon every tree will be dressed in
　white.
Oh, what a beautiful snowy sight!
Snow, snow, snow! We love it so!
Snow, snow, snow! We love it so!
Let's go outside now! Run, run, run!
Let's [catch a snowflake]. It's lots of fun!

Repeat, substituting the underlined phrase with
build a snowman, toss a snowball, and *take a sleigh
ride,* in turn.

Lucia Kemp Henry
Fallon, NV

Sprinkle, Sprinkle, Little Snow

Provide each student with two white crepe-paper streamers to twirl
and swirl as she sings about snow.

(sung to the tune of "Twinkle, Twinkle, Little Star")

Sprinkle, sprinkle, little snow;
Falling down on us below;
Small and white and powdery,
Such a joy for all to see.
Sprinkle, sprinkle, little snow;
Falling down on us below.

Linda Ludlow, Bethesda Christian School, Brownsburg, IN

Snowflakes Falling

(sung to the tune of "Kookaburra")

Snowflakes falling, falling to the ground,
Making a white blanket all around.
Snow on the house!
Snow on the tree!
Snow even on me!

LeeAnn Collins
Sunshine House Preschool
Lansing, MI

"Snow-key" Pokey

Have your little snowfolk form a circle; then get ready for a flurry of movement fun! To modify the verse, ask students to name additional pieces of winter attire. Keep warm!

(sung to the tune of "The Hokey Pokey")

You put your [mittens] in,
You put your [mittens] out,
You put your [mittens] in,
And you shake them all about.
You do The "Snow-key" Pokey
And you turn yourself around.
That's what it's all about.
"Snow-key" Pokey!

Gayle Selsback, Playhouse Nursery School
Maple Grove, MN

Think Snow!

Get youngsters thinking about winter fun with a song that also reinforces days of the week. There's a different activity for each day. Cool!

(sung to the tune of "Here We Go Round the Mulberry Bush")

What shall we do in wintertime,
In wintertime, in wintertime?
What shall we do in wintertime
On [Monday] when it's snowing?

We'll build a snowman round and fat,
Round and fat, round and fat!
We'll build a snowman round and fat
On [Monday] when it's snowing!

Sing the song again, using different days of the week and activities such as the following:
Tuesday, take a sled ride down a hill
Wednesday, find some food to feed the birds
Thursday, skate around a frozen pond
Friday, pack some snowballs round and tight
Saturday, make some angels in the snow
Sunday, build a snow fort in the yard

Cele McCloskey and Brenda Peters
Head Start of York County
York, PA

I'm a Little Snowflake

Visual discrimination and dramatic play drift into this snowy little tune. To enhance the song, have a small group stand as the whole class sings the song. Upon singing the last word, instruct each standing child to strike a "snowflake-y" pose and freeze. Then encourage their classmates to describe the similarities and differences among the snowflake children. At another time, have each child make a snowflake from art supplies (see an example above). Sing the song again, encouraging children to dramatize the song with their snowflakes. After each round of singing, encourage children to verbalize the similarities and differences among two or three of the crafted snowflakes. Even though you're at school, it feels like a snow day!

(sung to the tune of "I'm a Little Teapot")

I'm a little snowflake,
Look at me!
No other snowflake is exactly like me.
I am so unique, as you can see.
And just as special as I can be!

Bonnie Elizabeth Vontz
Ansonia, CT

I'm a Little Snowman

*(sung to the tune of "I'm a Little
Teapot")*

I'm a little snowman, short and stout,
Sticks for arms and a carrot snout.
When the weather warms up, gosh,
   oh gee!
I melt and there's no more of me!

Jan Payne
Dodge County Even Start Program
Eastman, GA

I'm a Little Snowman

(sung to the tune of "I'm a Little Teapot")

I'm a little snowman,
Short and fat.
Here is my nose
And here is my hat.
When the sun comes out,
I melt away.
But when it's cold,
I'm here to stay!

Markanne Gantt-Larberg, First Presbyterian Day School
Deland, FL

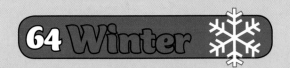

Five Silly Snowpals!

What might five silly snowpals do on a very cold and windy day? This delightful possibility is sure to warm up your youngsters' imaginations!

Five silly snowpals on a big hill sat.	*Hold up five fingers.*
The first one said, "I've lost my hat!"	*Touch top of head.*
The second one said, "My scarf's gone, too."	*Touch neck.*
The third one said, "Away they blew!"	*Sway from side to side.*
The fourth one said, "It's cold as ice."	*Wrap arms around self.*
The fifth one said, "Inside it's nice!"	*Point away from self.*
So they marched indoors;	*March in place.*
Then they cried, "We forgot!	*Place hands on cheeks.*
Inside it is much too hot!"	*Fan self.*

Five Little Snowmen

Have youngsters recite this poem using their own five little fingers as snowmen.

[Five] little snowmen
Went out to play,
Over the hills
And far away.
When the sun came out,
It melted one away.
[Four] little snowmen came back that
    day.

Repeat the poem, replacing the underlined number words appropriately. When you get to zero, use the stanza below.

[Zero] little snowmen
Went out to play,
Over the hills
And far away.
But when winter came back,
It brought snow along the way.
Then [five] little snowmen
Came back that day!

Andrea Esposito, VA Child Care Center, Brooklyn, NY

Sing a Song of Snowmen

Have each child play the part of a frosty snowman with this song and snowman mask. To make one mask, cut out two eyeholes from a white paper plate. Add a black construction paper hat and an orange paper nose. Use a black marker to draw a dotted mouth and then tape a jumbo craft stick to the back. Have each child hold her mask and sing the following song. Frosty would be so pleased!

(sung to the tune of "I'm a Little Teapot")

I'm a little snowman,
Round and fat,
With an orange nose
And a big black hat.
I like to be outside
On a snowy day
Until the sun
Melts me away!

Sarah Booth
Messiah Nursery School
South Williamsport, PA

I'm a Little Penguin

If you're looking for a penguin tune, here's one that will hit the spot.

(sung to the tune of "I'm a Little Teapot")

I'm a little penguin.
Look at me,
Fishing and swimming
In the deep blue sea.
My wings are black
And my tail is white.
And I like sliding down the snow so bright!

Daphne L. Rivera
Bob Sikes Elementary School
Crestview, FL

Penguin Play

Your little ones will learn a lot about penguins with this lively song. If desired, have students use penguin cutouts to perform the Antarctic antics.

(sung to the tune of "A Tisket, A Tasket")

Waddle, waddle!
Penguins like to waddle.
They have wings, but they don't fly.
Penguins only waddle.

Swimming, swimming!
Penguins all love swimming.
They catch fish and swim all day.
Penguins all love swimming.

Sliding, sliding!
Penguins all go sliding.
They slide on ice and snow all day.
Penguins all go sliding.

Sandy Moons
Park Crest E. C. E.
Long Beach, CA

A Penguin's Wish

This tune will help your little ones remember that penguins can't fly. Teach them the accompanying motions and have a waddling good time!

(sung to the tune of "I'm a Little Teapot")

I'm a little penguin, black and white.
   Point to yourself.

I'm good at swimming, but not at flight.
   Make swimming motions; then shake head to say no.

When I'm in the ocean, I dive for fish.
   Make diving motion with one hand.

Swimming's fun, but flying's my wish!
   Hook thumbs and wiggle fingers like wings.

Jean Zeller
WCSS St. William Campus, Waukesha, WI

Penguin Action

Set to music, this penguin poem becomes a miniature musical! Invite five youngsters to waddle up to the front of the class and pretend to be penguins. Then play a lively instrumental recording as you recite the poem. Direct each little penguin to play his part as directed in the poem. Repeat the activity until each child has had a chance to play the part of a penguin. With this Antarctic activity, your youngsters will soon be ready for "Brr-oadway"!

Five little penguins standing on the shore.
One dove in and then there were four.
Four little penguins sliding down, "Whee!"
One went too far and then there were three.
Three little penguins don't know what to do.

One waddled off and then there were two.
Two little penguins having lots of fun.
One went home and then there was one.

One little penguin sitting in the sun.
He/She went to sleep.
Now the penguin song is done!

Stand like penguins.
One swims away.
Wiggle hands above head.
One "slides" back to seat.
Shrug shoulders; look at each other.
One waddles back to seat.
Clap hands and cheer.
One waddles away and waves good-bye.
Sit down.
Pretend to fall asleep.

Cathy Seibel, Head Start, Greensburg, PA

Dr. King's Dream

Have youngsters join hands as they recite this meaningful poem about Martin Luther King Jr.'s message of kindness.

Hand in hand across the land,
For Martin's dream we choose to stand.
We say it loud, we say it clear,
"Peace and love throughout the year!"

Shandella Chapman
Butte County Head Start
Oroville, CA

A Melody for Martin Luther King Jr.

Have your youngsters honor Dr. King with the following song.

(sung to the tune of "Mary Had a Little Lamb")

Dr. Martin Luther King,
Dr. King, Dr. King!
Dr. Martin Luther King—
He was a loving man.

He loved all children everywhere,
Everywhere, everywhere!
He loved all children everywhere.
He was a loving man.

He had a dream for you and me,
You and me, you and me.
He had a dream for you and me
That we will live in peace.

Happy birthday, Dr. King,
Dr. King, Dr. King!
Happy birthday, Dr. King!
We will remember you.

Audrey Slater, The Betty Shabbaz School , Brooklyn, NY

Five Little Astronauts

In 1992, Dr. Mae Jemison became the first Black American woman to explore outer space. During Black History Month (February), teach youngsters about Dr. Jemison's accomplishments; then perform the following fingerplay in her honor!

Five little astronauts floating in outer space,
The first one said, "Let's get out of this place!"
The second one said, "Let's race to the moon."
The third one said, "We'll be there soon."
The fourth one said, "The space shuttle's ready!"
The fifth one said, "Now, hold it steady."
Then, ZOOM, they took off and started their flight,
And five little astronauts flew out of sight!

adapted from a fingerplay by Renee Farrand
Union Methodist Church Preschool
Irmo, SC

Healthy Teeth Tune

Smile! February is National Children's Dental Health Month. Have youngsters polish their toothbrushing techniques by acting out this tune!

(sung to the tune of "Here We Go Round the Mulberry Bush")

This is the way we brush our teeth,
Brush our teeth, brush our teeth!
This is the way we brush our teeth,
Morning, noon, and night!

We brush them up.
We brush them down.
Up and down!
Up and down!
We brush them up.
We brush them down.
Morning, noon, and night!

Beverly Russo
St. Margaret's–McTernan School
Waterbury, CT

Happy Teeth!

Plan to gather your little ones for this fun fingerplay, which highlights important tips for taking care of teeth!

Take care of your teeth and treat them right.   *Smile and point to teeth.*
Brush them in the morning and again at night.   *Pretend to brush teeth.*
When you go to the dentist, you can say,   *Walk in place.*
"I brush my teeth two times a day!"   *Hold up two fingers.*

adapted from an idea by Ellen Butorac
Fairlawn Village Preschool, Fairlawn, OH

Toothbrush Cha-Cha

Invite youngsters to dance along to this lively tune.

(sung to the tune of "La Cucaracha")

We brush our teeth up.
We brush our teeth down.
We brush 'em, brush 'em, all around.

We don't want cavities.
Oh, no, no gum disease.
We tell those germs, "Get outta town!"

Stand and pretend to brush teeth.
Squat and pretend to brush teeth.
*Stand again and pretend to brush
    teeth as you turn around in a circle.*
Shake head no.
Shake finger no-no.
Point thumb over shoulder.

Leslie Madalinski
Weekday Children's Center, Naperville, IL

Use Your Toothbrush

(sung to the tune of "Where Is Thumbkin?")

Use your toothbrush.
Use your toothbrush.
Every day,
Every day.
Keep your smile shining bright
Morning, noon, and every night.
Brush, brush, brush.
Brush, brush, brush.

LeeAnn Collins
Sunshine House Preschool, Lansing, MI

Two Little Groundhogs

Celebrate Groundhog Day (February 2) with this fine fingerplay.

Two little groundhogs in a burrow so deep
Stick out their heads to take a peek.
They look to the left.
They look to the right.
They hide from their shadows in the bright sunlight!

Make fists with thumbs inside.
Stick out thumbs from fists.
Move thumbs left.
Move thumbs right.
Pull thumbs back inside fists.

LeeAnn Collins
Sunshine House Preschool
Lansing, MI

Sleepy Little Groundhog

Take note of Groundhog Day with this action poem.

Up through the ground,
Creep, creep, creep—

The sleepy little groundhog
Peek-peek-peeks.

If he sees his shadow
And the sun is bright,

He jumps down his hole
And ducks out of sight!

Up through the ground,
Creep, creep, creep—

The sleepy little groundhog
Peek-peek-peeks.

If there is no shadow
And the clouds hide the sun,

He jumps out of his hole
And he's ready for fun!

Roxie Summers
Jack and Jill Pre-school, Leavenworth, KS

Rise and Shine, Little Groundhog!

On Groundhog Day have each child make a paper bag groundhog puppet to act out this simple song.

(sung to the tune of "Are You Sleeping?")

Little groundhog,
Little groundhog,
Sleeping all
Winter long.
Come out of your burrow.
Do you see your shadow?
Is spring near?
Is spring near?

adapted from a song by LeeAnn Collins
Sunshine House Preschool
Lansing, MI

It's Shadow Time!

(sung to the tune of "The Itsy-Bitsy Spider")

The furry, little groundhog
Goes in his hole to sleep;
Through the cold winter's
Snow and ice so deep.

In February,
He stretches to and fro.
Does the furry, little groundhog
Get scared by his shadow?

A Pretty Valentine

(sung to the tune of "Did You Ever See A Lassie?")

I have a pretty valentine,
A valentine, a valentine.
I have a pretty valentine
I'm sending to you.

It's red and it's lacy!
I made it so fancy!

I have a pretty valentine
I'm sending to you.

LeeAnn Collins
Sunshine House Preschool
Lansing, MI

Valentine Time

It's February! Time to bring out the valentines! Provide each child with a heart cutout or valentine card. Sing the song below and encourage your little sweethearts to position their valentines as directed.

(sung to the tune of "The Farmer in the Dell")

The valentines are here.
The valentines are there.
Hi-ho, the valentines are here and
    everywhere.
The valentines are up.
The valentines are down.
Hi-ho, the valentines are all around the
    town.
The valentines are in.
The valentines are out.
Hi-ho, the valentines are scattered all
    about.
The valentines are low.
The valentines are high.
Hi-ho, the valentines wave and say
    good-bye!

Jennifer M. Koch, Morningside College Child Care Center, Sioux City, IA

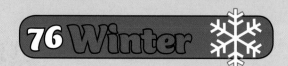

I'll Send You A Letter

If you're looking for a way to practice name recognition, this first-class game really delivers! Personalize an envelope for every child. If desired, tuck a small treat—such as a valentine or stickers—inside each envelope. Also locate a real or dramatic-play mailbox near your group area. To begin, hand an envelope to a child in the group. Instruct her to put the envelope in the mailbox as the group sings the first and second verses of the following song. Appoint a volunteer postal worker to remove the envelope from the box, and to deliver it to the appropriate child as the group sings the third verse. Continue until each child has delivered and received a letter.

(sung to the tune of "For He's a Jolly Good Fellow")

I'll send you a letter.
I'll send you a letter.
I'll send you a letter.
This letter is to [child's name].

I'll put it in the mailbox.
I'll put it in the mailbox.
I'll put it in the mailbox.
This letter is to [child's name].

I'll bring you a letter.
I'll bring you a letter.
I'll bring you a letter.
This letter is to [child's name].

adapted from a song by
D. Lyn Stevens
A.M. Chaffee School
Oxford, MA

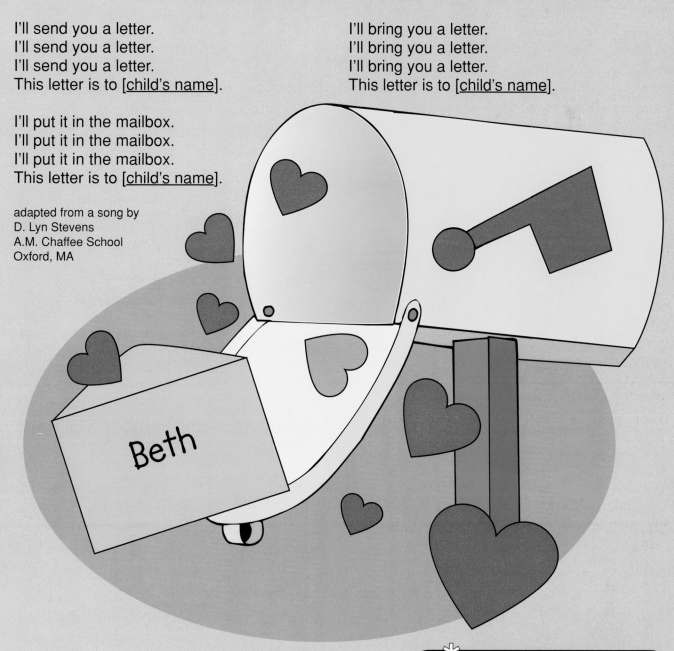

Will You Be Mine?

This simple song will have youngsters asking, "Will you be my valentine?"

(sung to the tune of "Clementine")

February, February, time to make a valentine.
Will you send one, give a friend one?
I will be yours if you'll be mine!

Nancy Cropper
James E. Moss Elementary
Murray, UT

Hearts in Hands

After youngsters learn this fingerplay, they'll want to make heaps of hearts! So follow up the fingerplay by providing a variety of materials such as pipe cleaners, thin strips of paper, and glue sticks. Then lead youngsters to discover that this heart poem works for making all kinds of hearts!

Now's the time to make a heart.
Form a V—it's the place to start.
A big hump on one side,
And now another.
This heart shows the love we have
for each other!

LeeAnn Collins
Sunshine House Preschool
Lansing, MI

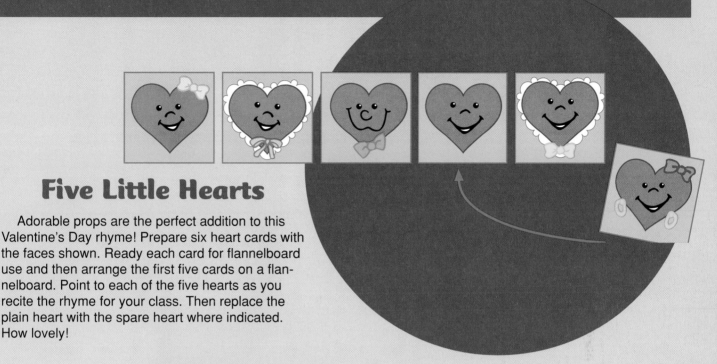

Five Little Hearts

Adorable props are the perfect addition to this Valentine's Day rhyme! Prepare six heart cards with the faces shown. Ready each card for flannelboard use and then arrange the first five cards on a flannelboard. Point to each of the five hearts as you recite the rhyme for your class. Then replace the plain heart with the spare heart where indicated. How lovely!

Five little hearts resting in a row.
The first one said, "I have a pink bow."
The second one said, "I have ribbon and lace."
The third one said, "I have a silly face!"

The fourth one said, "I'm plain as can be."
The fifth one said, "Just wait and see."
Then they dressed her up in a lovely way!
Five fancy hearts on Valentine's Day.

Candy Conversations

Sprinkle some print awareness in your Valentine's Day festivities! Label colorful heart cutouts with different three-syllable messages. Show students a message, read it, and then sing this song about it. Now that's a conversation heart chorus!

(sung to the tune of "If You're Happy and You Know It")

Oh, my conversation heart says "[You are nice!]"
Oh, my conversation heart says "[You are nice!]"
What a special thing to say on this loving holiday.
Oh, my conversation heart says "[You are nice!]"

Made With Love

This valentine chant and game will fill your circle time with love! Have each child color a personalized heart shape. Seat youngsters in a circle; then direct them to pass one of the hearts around the circle as they chant. When the chant is over, ask the child holding the heart to say something sweet about the child whose name is on that heart.

If you're feeling really sweet,
Make a heart that's nice and neat.
Add some kisses and a hug;
A valentine is made with love!

Carrie Lacher
Friday Harbor, WA

Will You Be Mine?

This colorful song and activity reinforces color recognition! To prepare, cut out a class supply of red, pink, and white construction paper hearts. Next, make a miniature mailbox by covering a shoebox with colored Con-Tact® paper and then cutting a slot in the lid. To begin the activity, provide each child with a construction paper heart. Then direct each student to place his valentine in the box when the color is mentioned in the song.

(sung to the tune of "Mary Had a Little Lamb")

Mail your [red] heart valentines,
Valentines, valentines!
Mail your [red] heart valentines,
And send love, oh so fine!

Repeat, replacing the underlined word with *pink* and *white* in turn.

I mailed my friend a valentine,
Valentine, valentine!
I mailed my friend a valentine,
And sent my love so fine!

LeeAnn Collins
Mason, MI

Pickin' Out Valentines

Here's a musical activity that's sure to make your little ones feel loved! In advance, cut out a paper heart for each child. Gather your youngsters and have them form a circle. Scatter the supply of paper hearts around the outside of the circle. Teach youngsters the following song. As they sing, designate one child to walk around the outside of the circle, select a paper heart, and then hand it to one of her classmates. In the last line of the song, fill in the name of the child who receives the heart. Then have the class sing the verse again as the recipient walks around the circle, chooses a heart, and then gives it to another child. Continue until everyone has received a valentine heart.

(sung to the tune of "The Paw Paw Patch")

Pickin' out valentines to give to all my friends,
Pickin' out valentines to give to all my friends,
Pickin' out valentines to give to all my friends,
Look! Here's one for [child's name]!

LeeAnn Collins

Spring

Leprechaun, Leprechaun

Your little leprechauns will have a high time moving to this spritely chant!

(chanted to the rhythm of "Teddy Bear, Teddy Bear")

Leprechaun, leprechaun,
Turn around.

Leprechaun, leprechaun,
Touch the ground.

Leprechaun, leprechaun,
Point to your ears.

Leprechaun, leprechaun,
Touch your beard.

Leprechaun, leprechaun,
Tip your cap.

Leprechaun, leprechaun,
Clap, clap, clap.

Leprechaun, leprechaun,
Dance a jig.

Leprechaun, leprechaun,
Smile so big!

Lucky Leprechaun

Your wee ones will enjoy singing this lively leprechaun song!

(sung to the tune of "The Itsy-Bitsy Spider")

The little leprechaun went skipping 'cross the ground.
He found a four-leaf clover with petals all around.
He made a secret wish that his day be filled with joy.
Then he ran to share his luck with every girl and boy!

Stephen Jobe
Greensboro, NC

Shamrock Search!

Prompt a shamrock search with this St. Patrick's Day song! Scatter on the floor a class supply of shamrock cutouts and a few distractor shapes such as hearts and circles. Sing the song with your class.

(sung to the tune of "I'm a Little Teapot")

Can you find a shamrock on the floor?
It has three leaves, but no more!
When you find a shamrock, you may say,
"This will be my lucky day!"

Linda Gordetsky
Palenville, NY

Five Little Leprechauns

Five little leprechauns playing in the sun.

The first one said,
"Oh, my! We're having fun!"

The second one said,
"We need to spread some joy!"

The third one said,
"Let's find some girls and boys."

The fourth one said,
"There's gold to be found!"

The fifth one said,
"Let's look all around!"

Then out came a rainbow,
Shining bright and bold.

So, five little leprechauns
Ran to find some gold!

adapted from a poem by
April Lena Pace
Suffolk Kids Cottage
Brentwood, NY

Spring Has Sprung

Celebrate the arrival of the first spring blossoms with this sweet action poem.

Tiny blossom in the sun,

Soft and quiet, the only one.

Reaching up to sun and sky,

Stretching up its leaves so high.

Tiny flower, so bright and gay,

Fills my heart with joy today.

Carrie Lacher, Friday Harbor, WA

Welcome, Spring!

Seat your children in a circle; then teach them this seasonal song and its accompanying motions.

(sung to the tune of "Christmas Is Coming")

Up come the flowers. *Raise hands.*

Out comes the sun. *Form arms into circle above head.*

Hear the bees buzzing. *Cup one hand behind ear.*

Springtime has begun! *Fold hands together.*

Up in the treetops *Raise arms above head like tree branches.*

The birds are all here. *Open and close hands like birds chirping.*

Now we know it's springtime. *All join hands.*

Let's give a great big cheer! *All stand and raise arms in a cheer.*

Spring, Spring, Spring!

Sometimes you just can't say it enough—spring is here! So invite your youngsters to serenade the season with this simple song.

(sung to the tune of "Three Blind Mice")

Spring, spring, spring.
I love spring!
I love the way the flowers grow.
Tulips! Daffodils!
All in a row.
Oh, so pretty!
I want you to know
That I love spring!
I love spring!

Arlea Kittredge
Arlea's Playhouse
Bowling Green, KY

Spring Is Coming!

Teach your youngsters this song with the accompanying motions. Welcome, spring!

(sung to the tune of "Frère Jacques")

Spring is coming. Spring is coming.	*Place hand above eyes and look around.*
Hear the birds. Hear the birds.	*Cup hand behind ear.*
They are busy finding They are busy finding	*Walk around looking toward the ground.*
Big fat worms! Big fat worms!	*Stretch arms out wide.*

Kathy Levy, Jacksonwald Elementary
Reading, PA

When Spring Comes Rolling In

(sung to the tune of "When the Saints Go Marching In")

Oh, when spring
Comes rolling in,
Oh, when spring comes rolling in,
[The flowers will all start blooming]
When spring comes rolling in.

Repeat, substituting the phrases below for the underlined words.

The plants will all start growing...
The birds will all start nesting...
The bees will all start buzzing...

LeeAnn Collins
Sunshine House Preschool, Lansing, MI

Fly, Kite, Fly!

(sung to the tune of "Up on the Housetop")

Up in the sky, I fly my kite
And hold the string with all my might!
Up in the sky, I fly my kite.
Up by the puffy clouds,
What a sight!

Fly, kite, fly
Into the sky!
Fly, kite, fly
Into the sky!

Up in the sky, I fly my kite.
Up by the puffy clouds,
What a sight!

LeeAnn Collins, Mason, MI

Spring

S is for *spring,* a wet time of year.
  Pretend to hold an umbrella handle.

P is for *puddles* of mud that appear.
  Wiggle hands in a pretend puddle.

R is for *rain* that falls on the tree.
  Ripple fingers down like rain.

I is for *iris,* the flower for me!
  Imitate sniffing a flower.

N is for *nest,* where eggs can be seen.
  Form a nest with hands.

G is for *grass* that grows tall and green.
  Stretch arms high above head.

Do You Have an Egg for Me?

During a group time, seat your children in a circle; then ask one child to pretend to be the Easter bunny. Give that child a basket filled with a class supply of plastic Easter eggs. As the group sings the following song, the bunny hops around the circle and then gives an egg to a classmate. This child stands up, puts the egg on the floor to mark his space in the circle, and then takes the basket for his turn as the bunny. Play until each child has an egg.

(sung to the tune of "He's Got the Whole World in His Hands")

Easter Bunny [child's name] is hopping by.
Easter Bunny [child's name] is hopping by.
Easter Bunny [child's name] is hopping by.
Oh, do you have an egg for me?

LeeAnn Collins
Sunshine House Preschool
Lansing, MI

Egg Hunt!

Add this quick poem to a classroom egg-dyeing experience for an "eggs-tra" dose of springtime fun!

Eggs aren't pretty when they're scrambled.
Eggs aren't pretty when they're fried.
An egg is only pretty when it's boiled and dyed.
You dip it into colors so it's one of a kind,
Then you hide it outside for a friend to find!

Little Rabbit Action Poem

Here's a little rabbit poem to keep things hopping in your classroom.

One little rabbit	*Hold up one finger.*
Underneath a tree.	*Hold arms up like tree branches.*
One little rabbit	*Hold up one finger.*
As "hoppy" as can be.	*Hop.*
Two long ears.	*Hold hands at back of head.*
Two big back feet.	*Raise and touch feet one at a time.*
One wiggly nose	*Wiggle nose.*
And whiskers so neat.	*Stroke fingers along cheeks.*
Two front paws.	*Hold hands under chin, fingertips down.*
Two eyes that shine.	*Point to eyes.*
One furry body	*Hug body.*
And a fluffy tail behind.	*Wiggle bottom!*

I'm a Little Bunny

Easter brings about bunches of bunnies. So teach youngsters the following tune and invite them to get hopping!

(sung to the tune of "I'm a Little Teapot")

I'm a little bunny.
   Point to self.

See me hop.
   Hop up and down.

Watch my ears go flippity-flop.
   Flip-flop hands like ears.

My tail is soft as cotton. Look and see!
   Pretend to wag tail.

My nose wiggles, so wiggle with me!
   Wiggle nose.

Jill Coakle
Generations Childcare
Rochester, NY

Cheep, Cheep!

Provide each child with a construction paper chick shape (similar to that shown) to decorate with markers and feathers. Then have each child put his puppet on his fingers. Hold your chick in a different direction each time you repeat the song and encourage your little ones to copy as they sing (and cheep) along!

(sung to the tune of "If You're Happy and You Know It")

If you have a yellow chick, say, "Cheep, cheep!"
(cheep, cheep)

If you have a yellow chick, say, "Cheep, cheep!"
(cheep, cheep)

If you have a yellow chick,
Hold it [up] like this, real quick!

If you have a yellow chick, say, "Cheep, cheep!"
(cheep, cheep)

puppet idea by Sue Jacobs, Shiloh U. C. C. Nursery School, York, PA

Chickie, Chickie

Have each child create a yellow chick by gluing together two yellow poms-poms and then adding wiggle eye stickers and a construction paper beak. When the chicks are complete, invite your youngsters to serenade their little chickies with this simple song.

(sung to the tune of "Did You Ever See a Lassie?")

Did you ever see a chickie, a chickie, a chickie,
Did you ever see a chickie so yellow and soft?
It peep-peeps and cheep-cheeps,
Then goes right off to sleep.
Did you ever see a chickie so yellow and soft?

Ada Goren
Winston-Salem, NC

Recycle!

Take note of Earth Day with this tune, which reminds everyone to recycle.

(sung to the tune of "Three Blind Mice")

Recycle! Recycle!
See how we save.
See how we save.
We save our paper, glass, and cans.
Everyone lend a helping hand!
We must pitch in to save our land,
So recycle!

Pauline Gould
Miami Gardens Elementary
Miami, FL

Earth Day Hooray!

Herald in Earth Day with this toe-tapping tune.

(sung to the tune of "The Ants Go Marching")

Soon it's gonna be Earth Day.
  Hooray! Hooray!
Soon it's gonna be Earth Day.
  Hooray! Hooray!
We'll do our part. We'll do our share
To clean up the earth everywhere.
That's what Earth Day's all about.
Give a shout! Say, "Hooray!"
  for Earth Day.

Ada Goren
Winston-Salem, NC

Three Little Raindrops

The forecast for this fingerplay calls for a downpour of fun with a 100 percent chance of learning!

Three little raindrops sitting in a cloud.

The first one said, "The thunder sure is loud!"

The second one said, "The lightning's very bright!"

The third one said, "A rainbow is in sight!"

Then splash went the raindrops, down from the sky

To water all the plants and help them grow up high.

Sharla Park
Friends and Neighbors Preschool
Lehi, UT

Mud Mix

April showers bring more than May flowers. They bring lots of mud! So teach youngsters the following action poem and get them in the mood for mud!

Mix the mud.

Squish the mud.

Squash it with your feet.

Squishy, squashy, squooshy mud.

Mud is really neat!

Make stirring motion.

Make squishing motion with fingers.

Stand on balls of feet and twist.

Pretend to make a mud pie.

Hold up hands, palms out.

For additional language play, repeat the poem replacing *squishy, squashy, squooshy* with *ucky, yucky, mucky.*

Lucia Kemp Henry
Fallon, NV

A Rainbow of Colors

Transform a few sheets of construction paper into a bright rainbow when little ones act out this tune. First give each of six student volunteers a different color of construction paper—one red, one orange, one yellow, one green, one blue, and one purple. Arrange the children in front of your group from left to right in that order. Ask them to hold their papers in front of them and then turn around so that their backs are to the group. As each color is sung, tap the child holding it and have her turn around and hold her paper high. Look! It's a rainbow!

(sung to the tune of "Pop Goes the Weasel")

Let's all name our colors right now.
Red and orange and yellow.
Green and blue and purple, too.
Look! It's a rainbow!

Deborah Garmon, Groton, CT

I'm a Little Umbrella

During those April showers, there's nothing more satisfying than popping open a big umbrella. Invite your youngsters to sing the following song in honor of the umbrella!

(sung to the tune of "I'm a Little Teapot")

I'm an umbrella.
Point to self.

I keep you dry
Point to "you."

When the rain falls from the sky!
Raise arms up; then wiggle fingers downward.

I have a sturdy handle
Pretend to hold umbrella handle.

And a curvy top.
Circle arms overhead.

Keep me up 'til the rain has stopped!
Maintain previous position; then put one palm out to gesture "stop."

Ada Goren
Winston-Salem, NC

Rhyme

For your youngsters, place a large sheet of
... marker markers in the six colors mentioned
... ne, draw an arc of each color. Ta-da—it's

Six little mar... ...ding in a line.

They said, "Let's draw a picture and make it mighty fine!"

Red jumped for joy as he leaped across the sky.

Orange jumped up too, but not quite so high.

Next came yellow as bright as the sun.

Green was excited as he started to run.

Blue followed boldly, then looked all around.

Purple came last, nearly touching the ground.

"Isn't this lovely?" the markers exclaimed.

"We've made a rainbow without any rain!"

Cheryl Cicioni
St. Anne Preschool at St. John Neumann
Lancaster, PA

The Itsy-Bitsy Seed

Teach little ones the accompanying motions to this tune. It'll grow on you!

(sung to the tune of "The Itsy-Bitsy Spider")

The itsy-bitsy seed was planted in a hole.
Pretend to plant seed in palm.

Down came the rain and a sprout began to grow.
Wiggle fingers downward.

Out came the sun and shone down on the leaves.
Place arms in circle overhead.

Now the itsy-bitsy seed is a great big grown-up tree!
Raise hands above head, fingers spread wide.

Kimberly Boston, Brooklyn Blue Feather Early Learning Center, Brooklyn, NY

A Planting Plan

Get all hands moving with this little ditty that reinforces the whole planting procedure.

(sung to the tune of "The Hokey Pokey")

You scoop the soil in.
You pick the rocks out.
You poke the seed in,
And you pat it all about.
You add a little water
And you wait for it to sprout.
That's what it's all about!

Debra Kujawski
Southold UFSO
Southold, NY

A Seed's Needs

Bring youngsters' gardening skills to the surface with this spring planting poem!

I plant a tiny seed in the dark, dark ground.
Out comes the yellow sun, big and round.
Down comes the cool rain, wet and slow.
Up comes a little plant—grow, grow, grow!

Pretend to plant a seed.
Make a circle with arms above head.
Wiggle fingers down to imitate rain.
Move hands upward.

I planted that seed in the dark, dark ground.
Now my plant is the tallest around.
It took a little rain and a lot of sun.
Who knew gardening was so much fun!

Point to the floor.
Reach arms to the sky.
Wiggle fingers; make a circle with arms.
Throw hands out with palms up.

Sprinkle, Sprinkle Little Seed

A little action combines with the rhyming lyrics of this song to help reinforce your plant studies.

(sung to the tune of "Twinkle, Twinkle, Little Star")

Sprinkle, sprinkle little seed.

Here is water that you need.

Down the sun is shining now.

Peek your head up; take a bow.

Sprinkle, sprinkle little seed.

Here is water that you need.

Jennifer Apgar, Messiah College
Grantham, PA

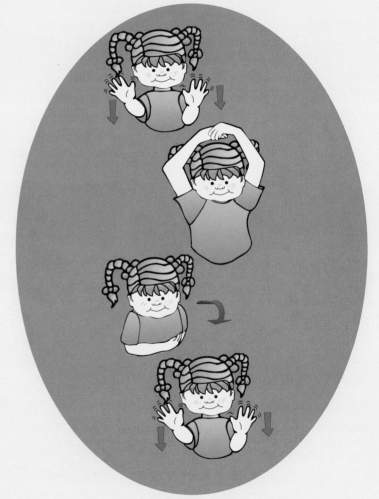

98 Spring

Hoe! Hoe! Hoe!

(sung to the tune of "Row, Row, Row Your Boat")

Hoe, hoe, hoe your garden
Up and down the rows.
See the [sun] come [shining down]
And watch your garden grow!

Repeat the song, replacing the
underlined words with *rain/pouring
down.*

Frances Easterling, Magee, MS

From Seed to Plant

Just how does a tiny seed turn into a tasty crop? Invite your little
ones to act out this catchy tune and they will quickly learn the farming
process.

(sung to the tune of "The Farmer in the Dell")

The farmer plants his seeds. The farmer plants his seeds.
Heigh-ho, it's planting time. The farmer plants his seeds.
The rain begins to fall. The rain begins to fall.
Heigh-ho, it's growing time. The rain begins to fall.
The sun begins to shine. The sun begins to shine.
Heigh-ho, it's growing time. The sun begins to shine.
The plants begin to grow. The plants begin to grow.
Heigh-ho, it's growing time. The plants begin to grow.
It's time to pick the crops. It's time to pick the crops.
Heigh-ho, it's picking time. It's time to pick the crops.
It's time to eat the food. It's time to eat the food.
Yum, yum, it's eating time. It's time to eat the food!

Cele McCloskey and Brenda Peters
Head Start of York County, York, PA

Over in the Garden

Help your preschoolers prepare for some springtime planting with this song. Ready, set, grow!

(sung to the tune of "Over in the Meadow")

Over in the garden with a rake and a hoe,
I'll plant some little seeds
In a nice, straight row.
"Grow," I will say. "Please grow all day long."
And the little seeds will grow
Into plants big and strong.

Lucia Kemp Henry
Fallon, NV

Five Dandelions

We're not "lion"! Youngsters are sure to have fun as they count down the verses of this dandy song.

(sung to the tune of "Five Little Ducks")

Five dandelions in the grass so green.	*Show five fingers.*
Little yellow flowers as pretty as you've seen.	*Make fist.*
One turned to fluff and then it blew away.	*Pop hand open; then flutter fingers away.*
[Four] dandelions were left that day.	*Show four fingers.*

LeeAnn Collins, Sunshine House Preschool, Lansing, MI

From April Showers to May Flowers

Little ones will enjoy performing this fingerplay from the month of April through the month of May!

Here come the April raindrops.
Wiggle fingers like falling raindrops.

They sprinkle and splash on my face.
Tilt head up and wiggle fingers over face.

Now here comes May.
Circle arms above head to form a sun.

The raindrops go away,
Wiggle fingers while raising arms up.

And flowers sprout up every place!
Pantomime picking and smelling flowers.

Three Little Tulips

It's true! This tulip tune reinforces colors, numbers, and measurement! Before teaching the song to your students, cut out three tulip shapes from white, pink, and red construction paper. Give one tulip to each of three children and have the youngsters stand in front of the class. As they sing the song below, direct one child to raise his tulip above the others. After singing, invite the class to identify the color of the tallest tulip; then repeat the activity with three different children.

(sung to the tune of "Six Little Ducks")

Three little tulips I once grew,
A white one, a pink one, a red one too.
One little tulip grew, grew, grew.
It grew taller than the other two,
The other two, the other two.
It grew taller than the other two!

Arlea Kittredge, Arlea's Playhouse
Bowling Green, KY

Flower Petal Countdown

Counting backward is a breeze with this song. Ask a child to stand in front of the class with his palm facing the group and his fingers spread apart. Explain that the child's hand is a flower with five petals. Instruct the child to bend down a finger each time the class repeats the verse. Get ready to blow the petals away!

(sung to the tune of "Sally the Camel")

[Child's name]'s flower has five petals,
[Child's name]'s flower has five petals,
So blow, wind, blow.
Blow, blow, blow…

[Child's name]'s flower has four petals…

Cheryl Sexton, First Baptist Day Care
Providence, OH

Happy Mother's Day!

Make plans for little ones to recognize mothers and other caregivers with a special serenade! To highlight another caregiver, a child simply substitutes his or her title in the opening line.

(sung to the tune of "Bicycle Built for Two")

Mother, Mother, you care for me night and day.
I know you are special in every way.
For all of the things that you do,
I love you and I thank you.
You are the best, so take a rest;
I know that it's way overdue!

Oh, When My Mom...

Moms and children will all feel special when you sing this Mother's Day song. Each time you repeat the song, ask a different child to supply a phrase to fill in the blank.

(sung to the tune of "When the Saints Go Marching In")

Oh, when my mom [gives me a hug],
Oh, when my mom [gives me a hug],
Oh, I know that I am special,
When my mom [gives me a hug].

Trish Draper, Millarville Community School
Millarville, Alberta, Canada

Bug Song

(sung to the tune of "If You're Happy and You Know It")

Oh, I wish I were an eensy-weensy spider.
Yes, I wish I were an eensy-weensy spider.
I'd go "creepy-creepy-crawly" down your hall and up your "wall-y"!
Oh, I wish I were an eensy-weensy spider.

Oh, I wish I were a yellow honeybee.
Yes, I wish I were a yellow honeybee.
I'd go "buzzy-buzzy-buzzy" and my stripes would be all fuzzy!
Oh, I wish I were a yellow honeybee.

Oh, I wish I were a wiggly caterpillar.
Yes, I wish I were a wiggly caterpillar.
I'd go "munchy-munchy-munchy." All the
  leaves would be my "lunch-y"!
Oh, I wish I were a wiggly caterpillar.

Oh, I wish I were a small red army ant.
Yes, I wish I were a small red army ant.
I'd go "trompy-trompy-trompy" over hills
  and through the "swamp-y"!
Oh, I wish I were a small red army ant.

Oh, I wish I were a hungry little skeeter.
Yes, I wish I were a hungry little skeeter.
I'd go "bitey-bitey-bitey" when you
  went outside at "night-y"!
Oh, I wish I were a hungry little skeeter.

Vicki Widman
A.J. Stepansky Early Childhood Center
Waterford, MI

How Do Bugs Move?

What's the buzz on insect movement? Find out when you point your antennae toward this active tune. As students sing the following song, have them move like the insects named. For added fun, provide your little bugs with headband antennae or paper wings. Students will buzz and float their way through this six-legged song!

(sung to the tune of "Bingo")

There was a little bumblebee,
Who buzzed around the garden.
Buzz, buzz, bumblebee.
Buzz, buzz, bumblebee.
Buzz, buzz, bumblebee.
Buzz around the garden.

There was a little ladybug,
Who crawled around the garden....

There was a little butterfly,
Who floated 'round the garden....

There was a little pesky fly,
Who zipped around the garden....

There was a little grasshopper,
Who jumped around the garden....

Dawn Spurck, Omaha, NE

Fuzzy Wuzzy Caterpillar

Your classroom will be bursting with butterflies when youngsters perform this action poem!

Fuzzy wuzzy caterpillar crawls along the ground.

Eating lots of grass and leaves,

He soon grows big and round!

He builds a house around himself.

Now can you tell me why?

'Cause soon you'll see him turn into

A pretty butterfly!

Cele McCloskey and Brenda Peters
Head Start of York County
York, PA

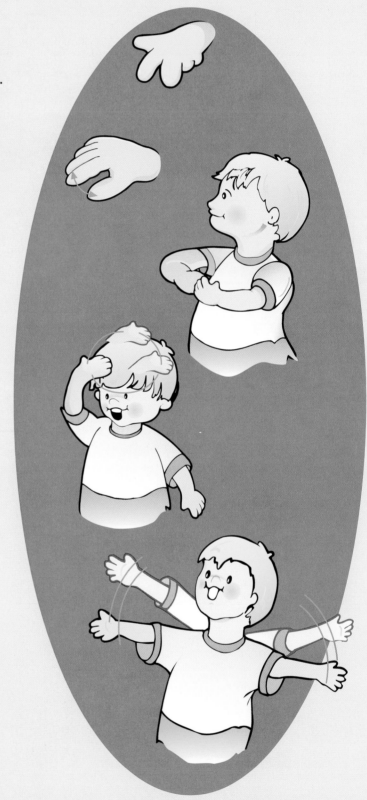

Once I Saw a Butterfly

Before teaching this tune to your students, die-cut a construction paper butterfly for each child. Laminate the butterflies and then staple a length of pipe cleaner to the back of each one. Twist each pipe cleaner to form a ring small enough to fit on a child's finger. Invite each child to slip a butterfly onto her finger and then use the butterfly to act out the following song.

(sung to the tune of "Twinkle, Twinkle, Little Star")

Once I saw a butterfly
Dancing in the clear blue sky.
Through the meadow he would go,
Flying high and flying low.
Once I saw a butterfly
Dancing in the clear blue sky.

craft idea by
Pauline A. Tomasek, Elyria, OH

song by
Diana Shepard, First Presbyterian Preschool
Wilmington, NC

Flitter, Flutter, Butterfly

Invite youngsters to use butterfly cutouts to accompany this song or, if desired, see the above idea for a puppet suggestion.

(sung to the tune of "Twinkle, Twinkle, Little Star")

Flitter, flutter, butterfly,
Flying in the big blue sky.
Flutter high and flutter low.
Flutter fast and flutter slow.
Flitter, flutter, butterfly,
Flying in the big blue sky.

The Buzz on Bees

(sung to the tune of "Three Blind Mice")

"Buzz, buzz, buzz,
Buzz, buzz, buzz,"
Said the honeybee.
Said the honeybee.
"I'm looking for nectar, as you can see,
To make some honey in my tree.
Honey that's yummy for you and me.
Buzz, buzz, buzz.
Buzz, buzz, buzz."

Janis Woods
Ridgeland Elementary
Ridgeland, SC

Surprise!

Delight little ones with this fun poem that bursts with springtime enthusiasm. When your students are familiar with the poem, have them recite it as they creatively act it out. Or, introduce the sign language for butterfly (see the illustration to the right). Then encourage children to dramatize the poem with their hands, ending with the butterfly sign.

I am a little caterpillar.
In my cocoon, I go to sleep.
And I won't move about for days.
You won't hear a single peep.
But I know I'll surprise you soon.
And do you know just why?
When the time is right for me,
I'll be a butterfly!

adapted from an idea by Patricia McIntyre
Beechwood on the Bay, Quincy, MA

Busy Bees

Here's a honey of a fingerplay! To make this fingerplay even sweeter, glue a craft bee to each finger on a right-hand glove. Then use the glove to perform the fingerplay. Buzz! Buzz! Buzz!

Five little bees	*Wiggle fingers on right hand.*
Up in the trees.	*Wiggle fingers above head.*
Busy,	*Wiggle fingers to the left.*
Buzzing	*Wiggle fingers to the right.*
Bumblebees.	*Wiggle fingers to the left and the right.*
First, they go to a flower.	*Hold left hand open; wiggle right hand toward it.*
Next, they go to the hive.	*Make fist with left hand; wiggle right hand toward it.*
Then they make some honey.	*Pat stomach.*
What a busy family of five!	*Wiggle fingers around.*

Donna Getzinger, Toluca Lake, CA

Where Are the Bees?

This simple adaptation of the traditional chant will keep youngsters giggling! Have each child cut a beehive shape from construction paper; then help her glue the top of her beehive to another sheet of paper. When the glue is dry, gently lift and fold back the beehive. Provide ink pads and markers for the child to make five fingerprint bees that will be hidden under the hive. Then lower the hive back down on the paper. Teach your little ones the rhyme below and have them dramatize it using their hives.

Here is the beehive.
Where are the bees?
Hiding quietly where nobody sees.
Are you sure?
Let's peek in the hive.
One, two, three, four, five...OUCH!

adapted from an idea by Leslea Walker
Ridgeway Nursery School and Kindergarten
White Plains, NY

Five Little Honeybees

This sweet fingerplay is sure to receive a swarm of compliments!

From a honeybee hive that's safe and warm,	*Hold up fist.*
Five little honeybees fly in a swarm.	*Open fist; then wiggle fingers.*
The first little bee gathers nectar from a flower.	*Point to thumb.*
The second little bee visits friends for an hour.	*Point to index finger.*
The third little bee packs the hive with honey.	*Point to middle finger.*
The fourth little bee finds a place that is sunny.	*Point to ring finger.*
The fifth little bee gets more than one chance	*Point to pinky finger.*
To practice the steps of the honeybee dance!	*Stand up and dance.*

LeeAnn Collins
Sunshine House Preschool, Lansing, MI

Two Big Beehives

What's all the buzz about? This summertime fingerplay!

Two big beehives
Closed up tight,

Hold out two fists.

Protecting sleeping bees
All through the night.

Rest head on hands.

When the morning sun
Shows its light,

Make circle with arms over head.

Ten little bees

Hold out two fists.

Take to flight.

Open fists and wiggle fingers away.

LeeAnn Collins
Mason, MI

This Little Ladybug

Youngsters are sure to enjoy "flying" these lovely ladybug finger puppets while singing the following song. To make one, cut a 2½" circle from red craft foam; then cut the circle in half to form wings. Use a black marker to add spots. Next hot-glue the wings, a bent four-inch length of black pipe cleaner, and wiggle eyes stickers to a film canister as shown. Ladybug, ladybug, fly away home!

*(sung to the tune of "This Little
Light of Mine")*

This little ladybug,
I'm gonna let it fly.
This little ladybug,
I'm gonna let it fly.
This little ladybug,
I'm gonna let it fly.
Let it fly, let it fly, let it fly.

Janis Woods
Ridgeland Elementary School, Ridgeland, SC

Great Grasshoppers!

(sung to the tune of "Jingle Bells")

Grasshoppers, grasshoppers!
They don't have a care.
Their strong legs push off the ground
And lift them in the air!

Grasshoppers, grasshoppers!
They can jump so high.
I love to watch them as they go
Leaping toward the sky!

Cynthia Holcomb
San Angelo, TX

Fireflies in Flight

Teach youngsters this firefly song and watch their faces light up.

(sung to the tune of "Camptown Races")

Fireflies come out at night.
Blink, blink. Blink, blink.
Showing off their little lights
In the summer sky!

Can you see them glow?
Flying to and fro,
Fireflies come out at night
In the summer sky!

Night Flyers

Easy-to-prepare moth props make performing this poem fun for all! Cut one 12-inch length of pipe cleaner in half for each child. Fold over each end to conceal its sharp edge. To make a prop, wrap the center of a pipe cleaner piece around your finger. Twist the two ends together near the finger and then bend each end into a wing shape. Make two moth props for each child and have her slip one onto each index finger before performing the poem. After the performance, collect the props and store them for future use.

Two little moths	*Hold up moths.*
Flying in the night.	*Wiggle moths.*
One goes left;	*Wiggle left-hand moth to the left.*
One goes right.	*Wiggle right-hand moth to the right.*
One goes up;	*Wiggle one moth up.*
One goes down.	*Wiggle one moth down.*
Then they fly around and around.	*Wiggle moths in circles.*
Two little moths	*Hold up moths.*
Flying in the night.	*Wiggle moths.*
They stop	*Stop wiggling.*
And they go	*Wiggle moths.*
Until the morning light.	*Rest moths on legs.*

LeeAnn Collins
Sunshine House Preschool
Lansing, MI

Spinning Spider

Spinning, spinning, round and round,

Little spider makes no sound.

Busy with her little spinner,

She hopes to catch a little dinner.

Old black flies and bumblebees,

Step right in now, if you please.

Busy with her little spinner,

Spider's caught a yummy dinner!

Cheryl Cicioni
St. Anne Preschool at St. John Neumann
Lancaster, PA

Let's Hear It for Frogs!

Sing this lively springtime song and invite youngsters to perform the froggy actions as directed. Now hop to it! Ribbit!

(sung to the tune of "Do You Know the Muffin Man?")

Oh, look! I see some [hopping] frogs,
Some [hopping] frogs, some [hopping] frogs!
Oh, look! I see some [hopping] frogs,
[Hopping] around the pond!

Sing additional verses replacing the underlined word with other action words, such as *dancing, croaking,* and *sleeping.*

Five Little Robins

Imaginations soar when little ones recite a poem about five baby robins ready to leave the nest. To make a hand puppet prop, glue felt decorations to the fingertips of a large brown garden glove to resemble five robins. Place the glove on your hand; then slip your fingers through a small grapevine wreath (nest). As you recite each line of the poem, wiggle the corresponding finger of the puppet.

Five little robins sitting in a nest,

The first one said, "I've had enough rest."

The second one said, "Let's fly from the tree."

The third one said, "That sounds good to me!"

The fourth one said, "I'm hungry for some lunch."

The fifth one said, "I see worms we can munch!"

So the five little robins all left their nest

To go and do what robins do best!

Sarah Booth
Messiah Nursery School
South Williamsport, PA

What Is It?

What hops, swims, and makes a "ribbit" sound? Little ones piece together the clues during this fun ditty!

(sung to the tune of "Do Your Ears Hang Low?")

Does it hop, hop, hop
'Til you think it will not stop?
Does it make a "ribbit" sound
On a day that's very hot?
Does it swim very well?
Then I know that you can tell
That it is a frog!

Linda Gordetsky
Palenville, NY

I'm a Little Froggy

Hop to it and teach your youngsters this little ditty! Ribbit!

(sung to the tune of "I'm a Little Teapot")

I'm a little froggy,
Slick and green.
I once was a tadpole,
As you have seen.
Then I grew some strong legs
While swimming about,
And now I'm a frog.
Hurray, let's shout!
"Ribbit!"

Cathie Rubley Hart
Westwood Hills Elementary, Waynesboro, VA

Ooo-eee! Slimy!

Do your little ones love slimy things? Ooo-eee! They'll love singing this slippery song full of similar sounds!

(sung to the tune of
"I'm Bringing Home a Baby Bumblebee")

I'm bringing home a slippery, slimy worm.
Won't my mommy wiggle and squirm?
I'm bringing home a slippery, slimy worm.
Ooo-eee! It slimed me!

I'm bringing home a slippery, slimy slug.
Won't my mommy shiver and shrug?
I'm bringing home a slippery, slimy slug.
Ooo-eee! It slimed me!

I'm bringing home a slippery, slimy snail.
Won't my mommy's face go very pale?
I'm bringing home a slippery, slimy snail.
Ooo-eee! It slimed me!

Lola M. Smith, Hilliard, OH

Our Friend, the Worm

Our gardens need worms! After discussing the benefits that worms provide, invite students to make these worm and flower props and then use them to dramatize the poem below. To make one flower, cut a flower shape from yellow construction paper. Then use a craft knife to cut a few slits through the center as shown. Turn the flower facedown. Apply glue around the rim of a foam cup and then press the cup down on the flower. Use a pencil to punch a hole in the bottom of the cup. To make a worm, wrap an adhesive bandage around the end of an unsharpened pencil. Then draw a face with a permanent marker. With a wiggle of the pencil, up pops a worm!

I was working in my garden.
I was clipping buttercups.
I was working in my garden,
When a worm just popped right up!

I looked at it and asked,
"What do you do?"
It looked back at me
And said, "I help you!"

Jane Wulf
Gainesville, FL

Summer

Summer

S is for summer, time to sip lemonade.
Pretend to drink.

U is for umbrella, giving us shade.
Curve arms up overhead.

M is for many hot days to go swimming.
Make swimming motions with arms.

M is for more baseball games to be winning.
Imitate swinging a baseball bat.

E is for everyone having lots of fun.
Pretend to laugh.

R is for red skin warmed by the sun.
Look up with eyes closed.

Let's swim!

Let's Give a Cheer for Summer!

(sung to the tune of "Bicycle Built for Two")

Summer! Summer!
Oh, I'm so glad it's here!
I love summer!
It makes me want to cheer!
What a warm and sunny season!
There isn't a better reason
For me to say,
"Hip, hip, hooray!
What a wonderful time of year!"

Kindergarten March

Remember that old, familiar army marching song called "Sound Off"? Use the call-and-repeat pattern of that chant to inspire youngsters to march right into celebrating the school year.

We can say our ABCs
And we know our one, two, threes.
We are learning every day
And this is what we have to say:

Count off—1, 2
Count off—3, 4
Count off—1, 2—3, 4!

We know all our colors too
And we can write our names for you.
We are learning every day
And this is what we have to say:

Count off—1, 2
Count off—3, 4
Count off—1, 2—3, 4!

Kindergarten's almost passed
But kindergarten was a blast!
We're still learning every day
And this is what we have to say:

Count off—1, 2
Count off—3, 4
Count off—1, 2—3, 4!

adapted from an idea by
Mary Anissa Chavers
Palm City Elementary
Palm City, FL

Preschool Pomp and Circumstance

When youngsters sing this song at your end-of-the-year program, parents will want to stand and cheer! In advance, have each child paint a picture for the program. As she sings the first three lines of the song, the child holds the painting behind her back. She holds up the painting as she sings the fourth line in the song and then brings it back down to sing the rest of the song.

(sung to the tune of "Take Me Out to the Ballgame")

We like [your school's name] Preschool!
Here we made lots of friends.
We learned our letters and numbers too.
Look! I painted a picture for you.
Let us root, root, root for our preschool.
Every day is so cool.
So, let's tell our moms and our dads
That we love preschool!

Cindy Quigley
Little Lambs Preschool
Corning, NY

Graduation Day

Cap off your graduation ceremony with a heartfelt rendition of this crowd-pleasing tune.

(sung to the tune of "Clementine")

Graduation, graduation,
Graduation day is here!
We had fun here at [school's name],
So let's give a happy cheer.

Now we're older. Now we're smarter.
We know some letters and numbers too!
For our teachers and our families,
We take a bow and say, "Thank you!"

adapted from a song by Jean Berweiler
St. Mary Nursery and Preschool, New Monmouth, NJ

It's Time to Say Goodbye

Use this tune to help end the year on a happy note! As a variation, substitute a different child's name for the words "our friends" in the first, second, and last lines. Repeat the song until you've sung a good-bye to each child in your group.

(sung to the tune of "If You're Happpy and You Know It')

Oh, it's time to say good-bye to our friends. *(Clap, clap.)*
Oh, it's time to say good-bye to our friends. *(Clap, clap.)*
Oh, it's time to say good-bye, so just smile and wink your eye!
Oh, it's time to say good-bye to our friends. *(Clap, clap.)*

Mark Pittelkow
Merrick Community Services Preschool, St. Paul, MN

Happy Trails

(sung to the tune of "Happy Trails to You")

Happy trails to you,
It's the end of our school year.
Happy trails to you,
Now summertime is here.
Next year we'll be in kindergarten,
But pre-k's the grade we left our heart
  in.
Happy trails to you,
It's time to say, "So long!"

Rhonda Leigh Dominguez
Oconee Pre-K at Downs Preschool
Bishop, GA

Kindergarten, Here We Come!

Let little ones show off what they've learned with this catchy end-of-the-year tune.

(sung to the tune of "Head, Shoulders, Knees, & Toes")

Learned my letters, A-B-C.
A-B-C!
Learned my numbers, 1-2-3.
1-2-3!
I can even write my name with ease.
Aren't you very proud of me?
Proud of me!

Kindergarten, here we come.
Here we come!
Kindergarten, here we come.
Here we come!
So long preschool, it's been fun.
Kindergarten, here we come.
Here we come!

Julie Iverson
Holy Family School
McKinney, TX

First Grade, Here We Come!

Help students look forward to first grade with this kindergarten review! Begin by asking children to discuss what they have learned in kindergarten; then record their ideas on a sheet of chart paper. Finally, display the chart and recite the poem below to celebrate a wonderful year of learning!

Look out first grade, here we come.
Kindergarten is all done!
We add, subtract, and read all the time.
Five cents is a nickel and ten is a dime.
We know many shapes and can tell time,
Plus opposites and words that rhyme.
Kindergarten is all done.
Look out first grade, here we come!

Susan McGhie, St. Ann School, West Palm Beach, FL

This Fabulous Year

(sung to the tune of "We Wish You a Merry Christmas")

We did a lot of playing,
We did a lot of building,
We did a lot of singing,
This fabulous year.

We did a lot of cooking,
We did a lot of eating,
We did a lot of sharing,
This fabulous year.

We did a lot of reading,
We did a lot of listening,
We did a lot of talking,
This fabulous year.

We did a lot of learning,
We did a lot of thinking,
We did a lot of growing,
This fabulous year!

Karen Hoover, Asbury Preschool, Raleigh, NC

Bubbles, Bubbles, Bubbles!

The next time you and your youngsters are blowing bubbles, sing this simple song to add to the fun!

(sung to the tune of "Twinkle, Twinkle, Little Star")

Bubbles, bubbles way up high!
Bubbles, bubbles in the sky.
Bubbles, bubbles way down low.
Bubbles, bubbles on my toes.
Bubbles, bubbles in the air.
Bubbles, bubbles everywhere!

Sherene Palmer
WMCAP Head Start
McConnelsville, OH

I'm Going Camping!

Prepare your young campers for an imaginary camping trip with this fun tune. As your children sing, encourage them to add motions to go along with the lyrics.

(adapted to the tune of "Twinkle, Twinkle, Little Star")

I'm going camping, yes siree!
I'm going camping; won't you come with me?
First we'll pitch our tent on the ground,
Then make a fire as we all gather round.
I'm going camping, yes siree!
I'm going camping; won't you come with
　me?

Next we'll cook on the open fire,
Then tell stories 'til we all get tired.
When the stars are twinkling bright,
We'll sleep in our tents 'til the morning light.
I'm going camping, yes siree!
I'm going camping; won't you come with me?

When we see the morning sun
We'll wake right up 'cause the day's begun!
There's so much that we can do—
Fishing, swimming, hiking too.
I'm going camping, yes siree!
I'm going camping; won't you come with me?

I Love to Hike Outside

Encourage your youngsters to think of all the fun summer activities they love to participate in by teaching this little ditty. Substitute students' suggestions by replacing the underlined word in each line. Yippee, it's summertime!

(sung to the tune of "She'll Be Comin' Round the Mountain")

Oh, I love to [hike] outside in summertime.
Oh, I love to [hike] outside in summertime.
Oh, I love to [hike] outside,
Underneath the sky so wide.
Oh, I love to [hike] outside in summertime.

Suzanne Moore, Irving, TX

Building Sandcastles

Youngsters build pretend sand castles as they sing this action song! Fortunately, no sand is required!

(sung to the tune of "Row, Row, Row Your Boat")

Dig, dig in the sand.	*Pretend to dig in sand.*
Pile it way up high.	*Pat a pretend pile of sand.*
Build a castle; make it tall,	*Shape a pretend castle.*
Right up to the sky.	*Alternate stacking one fist atop the other.*
Splish, splash, comes a wave	*Swing arms forward and back.*
And flattens out the sand.	*Pretend to flatten sand.*
Another castle must be built,	*Place hands on hips.*
And I will lend a hand!	*Enthusiastically raise hand.*

Linda Gordetsky
Palenville, NY

In My Swimming Pool

Here's a lively summertime song that will make a splash with your little ones!

(sung to the tune of "Do Your Ears Hang Low?")

I can stay real cool
In my little swimming pool.
On a sunny summer day
I can splash around and play.
When I wear my bathing suit,
I'll be cool and I'll be cute
In my swimming pool!

So Long, Seagulls!

Don't you just love watching seagulls take flight at the beach? Sing this song and invite your little ones to fly like a seagull!

(sung to the tune of "Down By the Station")

Down by the seashore
Early in the morning
See the flock of seagulls
All in a row.
See them flap their wings
And fly off toward the ocean.
Flap! Flap! Caw! Caw!
Off they go!

A Song for the Seashore

Did you know that a trip to the beach can be a stimulating experience for all five senses? This song will help your youngsters remember just how "sense-ational" the seashore is!

(sung to the tune of "Do Your Ears Hang Low?")

Feel sand in my toes.
Smell the ocean with my nose.
See the children splash and play
On a hot summer day.
Hear the ocean waves go ROAR
As they crash into the shore.
Taste the salty sea.

Karen Briggs, Marlborough Early Childhood Center, Marlborough, MA

Grand Ol' Dad

If you're planning a grand celebration for Father's Day, include this spirited song!

(sung to the tune of "Grand Old Flag")

You're a grand ol' dad!
You're a great guy, dear dad!
And forever in my heart you'll stay.
I love you so! Oh, don't you know?
I wish you Happy Father's Day!

Oh, my heart beats true,
Yes, I really love you!
And forever in my heart you'll stay.
I love you so! Oh, don't you know?
You're really a grand ol' dad!

adapted from an idea by Pam Fostano and Lisa Friesen, West Avenue School, Hilton, NY

Hooray for the USA!

Hip, hip, hooray! Your preschoolers are sure to feel patriotic when you teach them this Independence Day ditty!

(sung to the tune of "This Old Man")

USA! USA!
Say hooray for the USA!
On this fourth day of July,
Hold your head up high,
And say hooray for the USA!

LeeAnn Collins
Sunshine House Preschool
Lansing, MI

Hooray Red, White, and Blue!

Patriotism shows when your little ones sing this song honoring Independence Day. For added interest, tape one-foot lengths of red, white, and blue ribbon to the end of a craft stick for each student. Have youngsters wave their sticks as they sing the song below to create a beautiful red, white, and blue atmosphere!

(sung to the tune of "Yankee Doodle")

I love to wear red, white, and blue,
On Independence Day.
I'm proud to be American.
Hooray for the USA!
Happy birthday, USA!
I'll be true to you.
I'm proud to be American.
Hooray red, white, and blue!

Suzanne Moore, Irving, TX

We Love America!

Prepare your youngsters for the Pledge of Allegiance with this wonderfully simple patriotic song!

(sung to the tune of "Skip to My Lou")

We love America; yes we do!
To our country we'll be true!
Freedom is for me and you!
Hip, hip, hooray for the red, white, and blue!

Kellee Shuttleworth, Norwood Elementary School, Stonewood, WV

Shout Hooray for the USA

Celebrate the Fourth of July by teaching youngsters this lively song.

(sung to the tune of "If You're Happy and You Know It")

If you love the USA, [clap your hands].
If you love the USA, [clap your hands].
If you love the USA, [clap your hands] and say, "Hooray!"
If you love the USA, [clap your hands]!

Sing additional verses, replacing the underlined words with the following phrases: *stomp your feet, slap your knees,* and *do all three.*

Sarah Booth
Messiah Nursery School
South Williamsport, PA

Independence Day

Commemorate the Fourth of July with a patriotic sing-along.

(sung to the tune of "Jingle Bells")

Barbecues, swimming pools, picnics
    all around.
Stars and stripes are in our sights all
    around the town.
Look up high, in the sky—a fireworks
    display.
Celebrate the independence of the
    USA!

Linda Gordetsky
Palenville, NY

Picnic in the Park

Feel like having a summertime picnic? You will after teaching youngsters this poem!

Summer is the right time
To picnic in the park.
Let's eat lots of food
And stay out until dark!
Hamburgers and hot dogs
On the barbecue,
Corn and beans and pickles,
Potato salad too!
When our plates are empty,
We'll have something sweet—
Juicy watermelon!
What a picnic treat!

Lucia Kemp Henry
Fallon, NV

Here's the Scoop!

Ah! Ice cream! Need we say more?

(sung to the tune of "Camptown Races")

I eat it on a summer day.
Ice cream! Ice cream!
I eat it any kind of way.
I love to eat ice cream!
Scoop it in a bowl!
Scoop it in a cup!
Add some sprinkles to an ice-cream cone,
And I'll eat the ice cream up!

Lucia Kemp Henry, Fallon, NV

Pop, Pop, Pop

Sing this song quickly; then eat up those treats before they melt!

(sung to the tune of "Row, Row, Row Your Boat")

Pop, pop, pop on a stick,
A yummy frozen treat!
Cherry, lemon, orange, grape!
Cool and fun to eat!

Ada Goren
Winston-Salem, NC

Can a Watermelon Grow in My Tummy?

What's that? Someone swallowed a seed? Have no fear! The following song reminds little ones that a watermelon can't grow in there! Invite the children to echo you as you shout, "Oh, no!", then sing each verse.

Watermelon Echo Song

(sung to the tune of "Frère Jacques")

Oh, no! *(Oh, no!)*
I just swallowed *(I just swallowed)*
A watermelon seed. *(A watermelon seed.)*
Will I grow a watermelon *(Will I grow a watermelon)*
Deep in me? *(Deep in me?)*

Shout phrase, hands on face in alarm.
Begin singing slowly as with fear.

Oh, no! *(Oh, no!)*
That seed won't grow *(That seed won't grow)*
In my tummy. *(In my tummy.)*
There's no rain or sunshine *(There's no rain or sunshine)*
Deep in me! *(Deep in me!)*

Shout phrase.
Sing faster with joy.

LeeAnn Collins
Sunshine House Preschool
Lansing, MI

Guess What...Watermelon!

After singing the song, use the suggestions below to create new verses.

(sung to the tune of "London Bridge")

Guess what grows from small black seeds,
Small black seeds, small black seeds.
Guess what grows from small black seeds—watermelon!

Guess what grows with big green leaves...
What is round, and smooth, and green...
What's pink inside and full of juice...
What tastes sweet and makes me grin...

Leslie Ethington, Columbia, OH

Oh, Watermelon!

Before slicing into a watermelon, have youngsters serenade it with this song.

(sung to the tune of "O Christmas Tree")

Oh, watermelon, big and green,
You are the biggest that I've seen!
Oh, watermelon, big and green,
You are the biggest that I've seen!
Underneath the green and white,
You're juicy red. Let's take a bite!
Oh, watermelon, fun to eat,
You are my favorite summer treat!

Cynthia Holcomb
San Angelo, TX

Daily Routines

Terrific Transitions

To vary this song, simply insert the activity that's coming up and the desired action to make other verses.

(sung to the tune of "If You're Happy and You Know It")

If you're [ready to go outside], [pick up your toys].
If you're [ready to go outside], [pick up your toys].
If you're [ready to go outside],
If you're [ready to go outside],
If you're [ready to go outside], [pick up your toys].

If desired, sing the verse a second time, requesting another action on your students' part:

If you're [ready to go outside], [please line up].
If you're [ready to go outside], [please line up].
If you're [ready to go outside],
If you're [ready to go outside],
If you're [ready to go outside], [please line up].

Bonnie Elizabeth Vontz
Cheshire Country Day School, Milldale, CT

Come to the Circle

Help students make the transition to circle time with this lively tune!

(sung to the tune of "Take Me Out to the Ballgame")

Let's all come to the circle;
Let's all come right away!
We've got some sharing and learning to do;
There's so much fun right here waiting for you!
Oh, we've come to school for learning;
Everyone gather round!
And let's come, come, come to the circle and sit right down.

Rosalyn Harper-Jenkins, Marvin Elementary, St. Louis, MO

Sit-Down Snap

Use this chant and a steady string of finger snaps to encourage your students to take a seat for circle time. Repeat the chant until all children are seated. Snap, snap, snap!

1, 2, 3, 4—push in your chairs; then sit on the floor.
Make it quiet, make it snappy,
And you will make your teacher happy!

Sherri Martin
Southland Academy
Montezuma, GA

Look and Listen

Need to get your youngsters' attention? Here's a musical method for encouraging good listening!

(sung to the tune of "If You're Happy and You Know It")

If you're listening and you know it, look at me.
If you're listening and you know it, look at me.
If you're listening and you know it,
Then your eyes will surely show it!
If you're listening and you know it, look at me.

If you're listening and you know it, fold your hands.
If you're listening and you know it, fold your hands.
If you're listening and you know it,
Then your hands will surely show it!
If you're listening and you know it, fold your hands.

Karen Mayberry, Northside School, Morrison, IL

Keep 'em Clean

Keep this song handy throughout the year to remind students of a very healthful habit: washing hands! Soap and water ready?

(sung to the tune of "Row, Row, Row Your Boat")

Wash, wash, wash your hands
After work and play.
Scrub, rinse, shake, and dry.
Keep those germs away!

Clean Up!

This toe-tapping tune not only motivates little ones to clean up, but it also introduces some fun new vocabulary—spick-and-span. Explain to students that spick-and-span means spotlessly clean; then sing the song below and invite youngsters to get the room spick-and-span!

(sung to the tune of "The Muffin Man")

Oh, it's time to clean up now,
To clean up now,
To clean up now,
Oh, it's time to clean up now,
So everyone join in!

Let's make the room spick-and-span,
Spick-and-span,
Spick-and-span!
Let's make the room spick-and-span!
Now, everyone join in!

adapted from a song by Connie Nipper, Beebe Primary School, Beebe, AR

Time to Rest

Are your little ones sleepy yet? Set the mood for rest time by singing this song to your youngsters as they rest. Then name a different "nice thing" each time you repeat the second verse. Sweet dreams!

(sung to the tune of "The Wheels on the Bus")

Boys and girls, it's time to rest,
Time to rest, time to rest.
Lay your heads down.
Yes, yes, yes.
It's time to rest.

Dream a sweet dream while you rest,
While you rest, while you rest.
Think of [nice things].
Yes, yes, yes.
Dream while you rest.

Karen Eiben
The Kids' Place, LaSalle, IL

Good-bye

Settle your little ones and help them prepare for afternoon good-byes with this simple poem. Each day substitute the next day of the week in the last line of the poem. Then encourage youngsters to hug one another before heading out the door!

It's good-bye time, don't you know?
The time of day for us to go.
We worked; we played; we had our fun.
Now let's hug good-bye
'Til [Tuesday] comes!

Meri Visnic, Manzanita School, Kingman, AZ

"Name-O"

Help students recognize and spell their names and those of their classmates with this adaptation of a traditional tune. To prepare, write each letter of a child's name on a separate card. Have students stand in front of the group holding the cards to spell the child's name. Sing the song, chanting the spelling of the child's name in the third line. Sing about one child's name each day until every child has had a turn to hear her name-o!

(sung to the tune of "Bingo")

There is a friend who's in our class,
And [Jill] is her name-o!
Chant: [J-I-L-L], [J-I-L-L], [J-I-L-L],
And [Jill] is her name-o!

Dawn Hitt
Burnet Elementary
Burnet, TX

Alphabet Experts

Looking for a way to celebrate learning the alphabet? Invite your little ones to give themselves a pat on the back as they sing this catchy letter song.

(sung to the tune of "I've Been Working on the Railroad")

We've been working on our letters,
Learning the ABCs.
We've been working on our letters.
Just listen to us, please.

When you put letters together,
A word is what you'll get!
We will be terrific readers.
We know the alphabet!

Cindy Bowen, The Shepherd's Fold School, Hanover, PA

Alphabet March

Step to it and teach your youngsters an alphabet song they can sing while marching around your room!

(sung to the tune of "The Ants Go Marching")

A, B, C, D, E, F, and G.
H, I!
J, K!
L, M, N, O, P, Q, and R.
S, T!
U, V!
W, X, and Y and Z—
Now I've sung my ABCs.
And I've marched around the room,
round the room,
Round the room, round the room.
Boom, boom, boom…

Christy Brammer, South Point Elementary
South Point, OH

Letters and Their Sounds!

Here's an easy-to-adapt song that keeps students in tune with alphabet letters and the sounds they make! Before each singing, show students the letter they'll be singing about and review its sound. Tra la la!

(sung to the tune of "The Muffin Man")

Oh, do you see the letter [V],
The letter [V], the letter [V]?
Oh, do you see the letter [V],
For it says [/v/, /v/, /v/].

Oh yes, I see the letter [V],
The letter [V], the letter [V].
Oh yes, I see the letter [V],
And it says [/v/, /v/, /v/].

Linda Gordetsky, Palenville, NY

Letter and Sound Review

This playful review of a letter's name and sound is sure to become a favorite! To perform the song, provide each child with two stick puppets of the featured letter: one uppercase and one lowercase.

(sung to the tune of "Where Is Thumbkin?")

Where is [B]? Where is [B]?   *Hold puppets behind back.*
Here I am! Here I am!   *Hold up one puppet, then the other.*
Can you say the [B] sound?   *Wiggle one puppet.*
Can you say the [B] sound?   *Wiggle the other puppet.*
[/b/ /b/ /b/, /b/ /b/ /b/]   *Wiggle both puppets.*

Catherine Brubaker, Branch ISD, Coldwater, MI

A Verse About Vowels

This catchy tune will help your little ones remember the vowels!

(sung to the tune of "The Farmer in the Dell")

I know all the vowels.
I know all the vowels.
A, E, I, O, and *U*—
I know all the vowels.
Sometimes there is *Y.*   *Put hands above head to form a Y.*
Sometimes there is *Y.*   *Put hands above head to form a Y.*
A, E, I, O, and *U,*
And sometimes there is *Y.*

Tracy Gibas, John A. Sciole Elementary, Depew, NY

Vowels!

Remembering vowels is easy when students learn with this simple song.

(sung to the tune of "Bingo")

There was a classroom full of kids
Who knew the vowel letters.
A, E, I, O, U
A, E, I, O, U
A, E, I, O, U
And sometimes letter *Y* too!

adapted from an idea by Kristi Arndt
Lincoln HI Elementary
Hendricks, MN

A Very Fine Letter

Use this adaptable song to practice letter sounds! Show students the letter you're spotlighting and review the sound it makes. Then let the singing begin!

(sung to the tune of "The Bear Went Over the Mountain")

[R] is a very fine letter.

It couldn't be any better.

Let's sing about it together!

The sound of [R] is [/r/].

The sound of [R] is [/r/].

The sound of [R] is [/r/].

Oh, [R] is a very fine letter.

It couldn't be any better.

Let's sing about it together!

The sound of [R] is [/r/].

Linda Gordetsky
Palenville, NY

Tell Me

Use this song to focus on the elements of a story and then encourage students to retell a story from start to finish.

(sung to the tune of "Clementine")

Can you tell me?
Can you tell me?
Can you tell me about this book?
If you tell me all about it,
I'll be sure to take a look.

Who was in it?
What was happening?
Tell me how the problem's solved.
Retell the story from start to finish.
Tell me, tell me, tell it all.

Crystal Chandler, Wake Forest Elementary, Wake Forest, NC

In the Library

*(sung to the tune of
"Bringing Home a Baby Bumblebee")*

I'll walk very slowly in the library.
Won't Buddy Bookworm be so proud of me?
I'll walk very slowly in the library.
(Spoken) Ready? Let's tiptoe.

I'll talk very softly in the library.
Won't Buddy Bookworm be so proud of me?
I'll talk very softly in the library.
(Spoken) Shh. Let's whisper.

I'll put books on the shelf at the library.
Won't Buddy Bookworm be so proud of me?
I'll put books on the shelf at the library.
(Spoken) Okay, let's put our books away!

I'll check out a book at the library.
Won't Buddy Bookworm be so proud of me?
I'll check out a book at the library.
(Spoken) Now show me your library card.

The Crayons in the Box

Sing this colorful song to enhance students' color-word awareness. In advance, copy the song on sentence strips. Then label crayon cutouts with the color words from the song. Arrange all the word cards in a pocket chart. Sing the song several times together. Then, as you continue singing, invite students to take turns covering the color words on the pocket chart with the matching crayon cutouts.

(sung to the tune of "The Wheels on the Bus")

The crayons in the box are

Orange and blue,

Yellow and red,

Purple and green.

The crayons in the box are

Black and brown.

Colors all around!

Diane Parette
Durham Elementary
Durham, NY

Math

Crazy About Colors

Little ones will quickly learn to recognize colors with this song and activity. Provide each child with a set of crayons. After singing the last line of the song below, have students hold up the appropriate crayons and pretend to color.

(sung to the tune of "Paw Paw Patch")

Where, oh, where is dear little [red]?
Where, oh, where is dear little [red]?
Where, oh, where is dear little [red]?
Coloring the [apples] on the [apple tree].

Repeat, substituting the underlined words with other colors and phrases similar to the following: *yellow/lemons/lemon tree, orange/oranges/orange tree, blue/berries/berry bush.*

Louise Duval, St. Joseph School, Webster, MA

The Colors Song

Colors, colors, everywhere! Use this snappy little ditty to teach and reinforce colors in your classroom. Modify the words as needed by changing *wall* to *floor,* or by changing the color words. Then sing the song as youngsters participate in their daily routines and transitions. Before long, all of your little ones will be identifying colors all around the school!

(sung to the tune of "The Wheels on the Bus")

The colors on the [wall] are [yellow and blue],
[Yellow and blue],
[Yellow and blue].
The colors on the [wall] are [yellow and blue].
Find the color [blue].

Shelly Mace
Smithville Elementary
Smithville, WV

Twelve Months Make a Year

Here's a quick tune to help your students learn the months of the year.

(sung to the tune of "Clementine")

There are 12 months,
There are 12 months,
There are 12 months in a year.
January, February,
March and April, May and June.

July and August,
Then September,
Next comes fun October too.
Then November and December—
That's all 12 months. Now we're through!

Andrea B. Jané
Douglas Early Childhood Center
Douglas, MA

The Days of the Week

(sung to the tune of "Alouette")

Sunday, Monday,
Tuesday, Wednesday, Thursday,
Friday, Saturday; now we start again!

Sunday, Monday, Tuesday,
Wednesday, Thursday, Friday,
Saturday; now we're all done!

Pat Marr, Taft School, Ferndale, MI

Yesterday, Today, and Tomorrow

Reinforce these time concepts with your little ones every day as you sing this catchy tune.

(sung to the tune of "Mary Had a Little Lamb")

Yesterday was [Sunday, Sunday, Sunday].
Yesterday was [Sunday—Sunday]
    all day long.
Now today is [Monday, Monday, Monday].
Now today is [Monday—Monday]
    all day long.
Tomorrow will be [Tuesday, Tuesday, Tuesday].
Tomorrow will be [Tuesday—Tuesday]
    all day long.

Mildred M. Rodriguez
First Baptist CDC
Belton, TX

Musical Math

Reinforce number recognition with this musical math lesson! To begin, provide each child with a number card. Sing the first verse of the song below and hold up a number card for students to see. Then direct those students with a matching card to sing the second verse in response. Continue the song and activity until each child has had a turn to sing. When students are familiar with this call-and-response activity, adapt the song and cards to reinforce other basic skills, such as color, shape, or letter recognition.

(sung to the tune of "Short'nin' Bread")

Who has the number [one],
Number [one], number [one]?
Who has a number [one]
Just like mine?

I have a number [one],
Number [one], number [one].
I have a number [one]
Just like yours!

Carolyn Bryant
First Baptist Church
Powder Springs, GA

Counting Fingers

Keep wiggly fingers busy with this simple counting song! Have each child hold up ten fingers and then put one finger down when indicated. Pause to have children count how many fingers are left. Sing additional verses of the song, starting each one with the number of fingers that remain extended. Fabulous finger facts!

(sung to the tune of "Did You Ever See a Lassie?")

Show me your [ten] fingers,
[Ten] fingers, [ten] fingers.
Show me your [ten] fingers,
Now take one away!

Monica Saunders, Hazelwild Educational Foundation
Fredericksburg, VA

Ten on a Plate

Combine math and a snack for a tasty lesson in subtraction! Give each child ten small snack items, such as Goldfish crackers or cereal. Sing the following song and encourage each youngster to gobble up one piece at the appropriate time. Continue counting down until you reach the last verse. Pause after each verse and instruct students to quietly count how many pieces they have left. It won't be long before they'll be singing with you!

(sung to the tune of "Ten in a Bed")

There are [10] on my plate,
And the teacher says, "Wait!
Eat just one!
Eat just one!"
Pause while children chew.
So I ate just one.
Doing math is fun!
There are…

Final verse:
There are none on my plate,
And the teacher says, "Hey!
You're all done!
You're all done!"

Andrea B. Jané
Douglas Early Childhood Center
Douglas, MA

Sing a Song of Senses

Add a little song to your five-senses study with this catchy tune.

(sung to the tune of "The Farmer in the Dell")

We use our tongues to taste.
We use our tongues to taste.
We taste the flavors in our food.
We use our tongues to taste.

We use our ears to hear.
We use our ears to hear.
We hear noises loud and soft.
We use our ears to hear.

We use our eyes to see.
We use our eyes to see.
We see colors all around.
We use our eyes to see.

We use our noses to smell.
We use our noses to smell.
We smell flowers and perfume.
We use our noses to smell.

We use our hands to touch.
We use our hands to touch.
We touch things both smooth and rough.
We use our hands to touch.

Dianne Gleason
Preston Hollow Elementary, Dallas, TX

Sing a Song of Seasons

(sung to the tune of "Sing a Song of Sixpence")

Sing a song of seasons,

Something bright in all.

Flowers in the summer,

Leaves in the fall.

Snow in the winter,

Buds in the spring.

Aren't all these changes

A wonderful thing?

Joan Grohowski
Posen Homebase Head Start
Presque Isle, MI

Movement

Moving Hands

(sung to the tune of "Turkey in the Straw")

I can clap my hands,
Clap high, clap low.
I can clap my hands,
Clap fast, clap slow.
I can clap my hands to the left and the right.
I can clap my hands 'til I say, "Good night!"

I can wiggle my fingers,
Wiggle high, wiggle low.
I can wiggle my fingers,
Wiggle fast, wiggle slow.
I can wiggle my fingers to the
    left and the right.
I can wiggle my hands 'til I say,
    "Good night!"

I can snap my fingers,
Snap high, snap low.
I can snap my fingers,
Snap fast, snap slow.
I can snap my fingers to the
    left and the right.
I can snap my fingers 'til I say,
    "Good night!"

I can wave my hands,
Wave high, wave low.
I can wave my hands,
Wave fast, wave slow.
I can wave my hands to the left
    and the right.
I can wave my hands 'til I say,
    "Good night!"

Suzanne Moore
Irving, TX

Blast Off!

Ten, nine, eight, seven, six, five,
Four, three, two, one, blast off!

In my rocket ship I'll fly,

Up so high into the sky.

Touch a star or maybe two,

Even land upon the Moon.

And when I'm through, I'll turn around.

Instead of up, I'll then go down.

Heidi Barket
Eastside Christian Preschool, Pottsville, PA

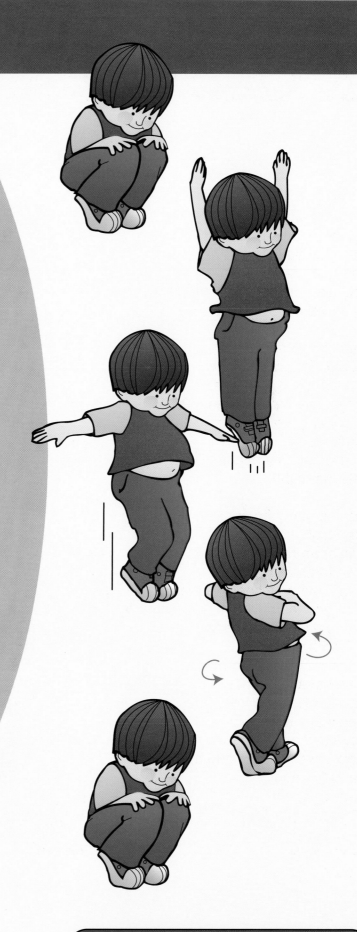

Dino Ditty, Ditty Dum Ditty Do

Here's a song that's a real blast from the past!

(sung to the tune of "Do Wah Diddy Diddy")

Here he comes just a stomping with his feet,	*Stomp.*
Singing "dino ditty, ditty dum ditty do."	*Clap.*
Searching all around for something good to eat,	*Hand over brow.*
Singing "dino ditty, ditty dum ditty do."	*Clap.*
He's huge. (He's huge.) He's strong. (He's strong.)	*Stretch out arms; then bend elbows and make fists.*
He's huge, he's strong, won't be hungry very long.	*Repeat arm motions; then shake finger "no."*
"Dino ditty, ditty dum ditty do…"	*Clap.*
"Dino ditty, ditty dum ditty do…"	*Clap.*

Marsha Feffer
Salem Early Childhood Center/Bentley School
Salem, MA

Wiggle Your Fingers, Stomp Your Feet

Use this movement poem to invite youngsters to wiggle and stomp right into your morning circle time.

Wiggle your fingers in the air.
Wiggle them, wiggle them everywhere!

Stomp your feet upon the ground.
Stomp them, stomp them all around!

Now sit down and cross your feet.
Hands in laps all nice and neat.

Now we're ready to start our day.
We'll listen first, and then we'll play!

Sandy Curtis
Browncraft Day Care Center
Rochester, NY

Tree Tune

Review the parts of a fruit tree with this fun action song! Each time children sing the word *leaves,* have them wiggle their fingers. For *branches,* have them sway their arms. For *trunk,* have them touch their tummies, and for *roots,* have them touch their toes. In Line 5, have students pause after the word *blossoms* to take a big sniff and pause after the word *fruits* to take a pretend bite!

(sung to the tune of "Head and Shoulders")

Leaves, branches, trunk, and roots,
Trunk and roots.
Leaves, branches, trunk, and roots,
Trunk and roots.
Don't forget the blossoms (*sniff*) and the fruits (*bite*)!
Leaves, branches, trunk, and roots,
Trunk and roots.

Suzanne Moore
Irving, TX

Get Shakin'!

This song is sure to have youngsters shaking, stamping, snapping, and clapping their way into group time.

(sung to the tune of "The Wheels on the Bus")

It's time to shake
And shake and shake.
Stamp and stamp.
Snap and clap.
It's time to shake and shake and shake.
It's time to sit right down!

Pigs on the Run!

Why are these pigs in such a hurry? Act out this poem and find out!

One piggy, two piggies,	*Hold up one and then two fingers.*
Three piggies, four	*Hold up three and then four fingers.*
Wag their tails	*Pretend to wag tail.*
And run out the door!	*Slap hands on legs to make running sound.*
Five piggies, six piggies,	*Hold up five and then six fingers.*
Seven piggies, eight	*Hold up seven and then eight fingers.*
Hurry 'cross the yard	*Slap hands on legs to make running sound.*
And jump the gate!	*Clap hands.*
Nine piggies, ten piggies	*Hold up nine and then ten fingers.*
Head down the street	*Slap hands on legs to make running sound.*
And go to the market	
For a sweet and tasty treat!	*Pat stomach.*

Eva O'Laughlin
St. Mary's School
Breckenridge, MN

Quack! Mew! Oink!

Give pictures of the baby animals mentioned in this song to your youngsters to hold. Have each child hold up her animal as its verse is sung. And invite everyone to make the animal sounds for every verse!

(sung to the tune of "She'll Be Comin' Round the Mountain")

Oh, a baby duck's a duckling. It says, "Quack." *Quack, quack!*
Oh, a baby duck's a duckling. It says, "Quack." *Quack, quack!*
All its yellow fluffy feathers keep it warm in rainy weather.
Oh, a baby duck's a duckling. It says, "Quack." *Quack, quack!*

Oh, a baby cat's a kitten. It says, "Mew." *Mew, mew!*
Oh, a baby cat's a kitten. It says, "Mew." *Mew, mew!*
Likes to chase and scratch and purr, licks itself to clean its fur.
Oh, a baby cat's a kitten. It says, "Mew." *Mew, mew!*

Oh, a baby pig's a piglet. It says, "Oink." *Oink, oink!*
Oh, a baby pig's a piglet. It says, "Oink." *Oink, oink!*
Mud's its favorite place to play…cools it down the fastest way.
Oh, a baby pig's a piglet. It says, "Oink." *Oink, oink!*

Oh, a baby horse is a foal. It says, "Neigh." *Neigh, neigh!*
Oh, a baby horse is a foal. It says, "Neigh." *Neigh, neigh!*
Spindly legged, runs so fast, likes to eat the farmer's grass.
Oh, a baby horse is a foal. It says, "Neigh." *Neigh, neigh!*

Oh, a baby sheep's a lamb. It says, "Baa." *Baa, baa!*
Oh, a baby sheep's a lamb. It says, "Baa." *Baa, baa!*
Soft and woolly, it will stay by its mother through the day.
Oh, a baby sheep's a lamb. It says "Baa." *Baa, baa!*

Michelle McCormick, Washington Elementary, Holdrege, NE

Farm 157

Five Spotted Cows

Teach youngsters the following poem about cows. Then invite five students to stand in front of the class and act out some bovine behavior.

Five spotted cows, standing in a line.
The first one said, "I'm feeling fine!"   *Point to self.*
The second one said, "How do you do?"   *Turn to third cow and hold out*
                                                                                    right hand.
The third one said, "Moo! Moo! Moo!"   *Take second cow's hand and*
                                                                                    shake it.
The fourth one said, "I'm grazing in the grass." *Make chewing motion.*
The fifth one said, "I'm full at last!"   *Pat tummy.*
So the cows stood together and said,
"We're through! Let's take a bow and all say, 'MOO!'"

Lisa Thayer
Bunche ECDC
Tulsa, OK

The Ins and Outs of Farm Life

Little Boy Blue may be sleeping, but your group won't be when it's their turn to let the animals in and out of the barn. To prepare for this singing game, use masking tape to make the outline of a square on the floor. Make sure that the square is large enough for your class to line up on its four sides to form the walls of a barn. Direct the children to stand on the tape; then give one child a plastic farm animal. As the group sings the first verse of the following song, the child walks around the outside of the barn. As the group sings the second verse, the child walks inside the barn. To continue, give another child a different animal, and have the group sing more about the ins and outs of farm life.

In and Out of the Barn

(sung to the tune of "The Farmer in the Dell")

The [animal]'s out of the barn.
The [animal]'s out of the barn.
Heigh-ho, the derry-o;
The [animal]'s out of the barn.

The [animal] is in the barn.
The [animal] is in the barn.
Heigh-ho, the derry-o;
The [animal] is in the barn.

In the Farmyard

Animal noises abound in this lively tune! Have your young farmhands sing it several times, substituting other animals and animal noises for the underlined words.

(sung to the tune of "My Bonnie Lies Over the Ocean")

The [cow] lives out in the farmyard.
She's an animal I go to see.
The [cow] lives out in the farmyard
And sometimes she says things to me.
["Moo, moo, moo, moo."]
That's what the [cow] says to me, to me.
["Moo, moo, moo, moo."]
That's what the [cow] says to me!

adapted from a song by LeeAnn Collins
Sunshine House Preschool, Lansing, MI

Animals

Do You See?

A wave of sea-related vocabulary washes in with this oceanic tune. As you sing, encourage your students to act out how each featured creature would look as it swims in the sea. After you sing the suggested verses, encourage children to brainstorm additional animals that might be seen in the sea. Then repeat the song, substituting a child-suggested creature each time. "Sea" ya!

(sung to the tune of "The Muffin Man")

Do you see [a jellyfish],
[A jellyfish, a jellyfish]?
Do you see [a jellyfish]
A-swimming in the sea?

Do you see a sea turtle…?
Do you see an octopus…?
Do you see a tiger shark…?
Do you see a sea urchin…?

Betty Silkunas, Lansdale, PA

Mr. Lobster and Mrs. Crab

Here's an ocean-related song with some fine-motor fun splashed in!

(adapted to the tune of "Old MacDonald Had a Farm")

Mr. Lobster and Mrs. Crab
Pinch and snap all day.
Mr. Lobster and Mrs. Crab
Pinch and snap all day.
With a pinch pinch here,
And a snap snap there.
Here a pinch,
There a snap,
Everywhere a pinch, snap.
Mr. Lobster and Mrs. Crab
Pinch and snap all day.

Betty Silkunas

Baby Alligator

 A baby alligator was green and small;

 He hadn't any sharp teeth, none at all.

 He snapped at a beetle, and he snapped at a fly.

 But he didn't catch a thing, so he started to cry.

 The baby alligator grew big and long.

 Soon his teeth were sharp and strong.

 Now he snaps at the beetle, and he snaps at the fly;

 He's a happy alligator, and we know why!

Carrie Lacher
Friday Harbor, WA

Get Those Gators Moving!

Your youngsters will grin like gators with this alligator song and activity. Guide students in performing the alligator actions in the song below.

(sung to the tune of "The Wheels on the Bus")

The alligator's [tail] go(es) [swish, swish, swish];
[Swish, swish, swish; swish, swish, swish].
The alligator's [tail] go(es) [swish, swish, swish]
Down in the swamp!

Repeat the verse, substituting the underlined words with *eye/wink, legs/splash,* and *jaws/snap.*

Little Joey

(sung to the tune of "Did You Ever See a Lassie?")

I have a little joey, a joey, a joey.
I have a little joey who lives in my pouch.
I jump up and jump down,
He bumps up and bumps down.
I have a little joey who lives in my pouch.

I have a little joey, a joey, a joey.
I have a little joey who lives in my pouch.
I jump right and jump left,
He bumps right and bumps left.
I have a little joey who lives in my pouch.

I'm a Little Turtle

Talking about turtles? Teach your tots this tune and then have them act it out!

(sung to the tune of "I'm a Little Teapot")

I'm a little turtle—
Oh, so slow.
I wear my house on my back, you know.
When it's time for me to go inside,
I tuck my legs and then I hide!

Jamie Stewart
J. F. Burns Elementary
Kings Mills, OH

Down by the Bear Cave

Your little cubs will pretend to fill up on tasty bear treats while singing this song. Sing the verses below, substituting other bear foods, such as termites and berries, in the second verse. A growlin' good breakfast!

(sung to the tune of "Down by the Station")

Down by the bear cave early in the morning,
See the little bear cubs all in a row.
See the mama bear; she's bringing home
    some honey.
Yum, yum! Chomp, chomp!
Down it goes!

Down by the bear cave early in the morning,
See the little bear cubs all in a row.
See the mama bear; she's bringing home
    some [fishies].
Yum, yum! Chomp, chomp!
Down they go!

Daphne L. Rivera
Bob Sikes Elementary School
Crestview, FL

Pet Care Chorus

Will youngsters enjoy this cute canine chorus? Yes, ma'am! To perform the song, sing the question at the beginning of each line. Then have students respond by singing the words in parentheses.

(sung to the tune of "Did You Feed My Cow?")

Did you feed my dog?	*Yes, ma'am.*
Did you feed my dog?	*Yes, ma'am.*
What did you feed her?	*Food, food, food.*
What did you feed her?	*Food, food, food.*
Did you wash my dog?	*Yes, ma'am.*
Did you wash my dog?	*Yes, ma'am.*
How did you wash her?	*Scrub, scrub, scrub.*
How did you wash her?	*Scrub, scrub, scrub.*
Did you walk my dog?	*Yes, ma'am.*
Did you walk my dog?	*Yes, ma'am.*
How did you walk her?	*Step, step, step.*
How did you walk her?	*Step, step, step.*

Sherry Hammons
Woman's Hospital Child Development Center
Baton Rouge, LA

Here Comes Tyrannosaurus Rex!

If your little ones are fascinated with dinosaurs, then teach them this fun fingerplay. But don't be surprised if, at the end, they all run away!

Five Huge Dinosaurs

Five huge dinosaurs, looking fierce and mean.
The first one said, "I eat things that are green."
The second one said, "I hatched from an egg."
The third one said, "I have big, strong legs."
The fourth one said, "I can fly through the air."
The fifth one said, "I give everyone a scare!"
THUMP, THUMP came Tyrannosaurus Rex that day,
And the five huge dinosaurs all ran away!

Linda Bockhorn
Kings Kids Preschool, Kings Local School District, Kings Mills, OH

Circus

A Mouse Can

Teach this mouse-movement poem to your youngsters, and they'll be following directions, practicing oral language, learning new vocabulary, and getting their wiggles out with every little squeak.

A mouse can twitch its nose.
A mouse can squeak, squeak, squeak.
A mouse can even hide
In the dark and take a peek!

A mouse can really dig.
A mouse can eat, eat, eat.
A mouse can scamper, scamper
On its four little feet.

A mouse can hop about.
A mouse can leap, leap, leap.
A mouse can snuggle up
In a ball, so fast asleep!

Take Me Out to the Circus

Delight your little ones with this circus idea! Use stickers or cutouts to create a class supply of stick puppets that match the animals named in the song. Have the children stand in a circle; then give each child a puppet to raise when his animal is named.

(sung to the tune of "Take Me Out to the Ballgame")

Take me out to the circus.
Take me to the big top.
Show me some horses and lions and
    clowns,
Monkeys and elephants dancing around.
Can you hear the band playing loudly?
We're ready and set to go!
Oh, I love, love, love the big top
And the circus show!

LeeAnn Collins
Sunshine House Preschool, Lansing, MI

Zoo

In the Zoo

(sung to the tune of "The Farmer in the Dell")

The monkeys in the zoo,
The monkeys in the zoo,
They bend their knees and swing from trees,
The monkeys in the zoo.

The zebras in the zoo,
The zebras in the zoo,
They look so right in black and white,
The zebras in the zoo.

The seals in the zoo,
The seals in the zoo,
They swim and splash the whole day through,
The seals in the zoo.

The lions in the zoo,
The lions in the zoo,
They lift their heads and give a roar,
The lions in the zoo.

The children at the zoo,
The children at the zoo,
They have such fun till the day is done,
The children at the zoo.

Elizabeth McDonald
School Readiness Center
Naperville, IL

Zoo Tune

Get little ones in the mood for the zoo with this lively song!

(sung to the tune of "My Bonnie Lies Over the Ocean")

I came to the zoo to see lions,
Elephants, tigers, and bears.
I came to the zoo to see zebras.
I love all the animals there!

Lions, tigers,
Elephants, zebras, and bears,
And bears!
Lions, tigers,
Elephants, zebras, and bears!

LeeAnn Collins, Sunshine House Preschool, Lansing, MI

Food

A Tasteful Tune

Teaching about nutrition? Teach youngsters this song! Before singing, discuss different healthful foods with your students. Then incorporate each food into the song below. What will youngsters think of this catchy nutrition tune? Oh, they'll eat it up!

(sung to the tune of "Boom, Boom, Ain't It Great to Be Crazy?")

Yum! Yum! Don't you love to eat [green beans]?
Yum! Yum! Don't you love to eat [green beans]?
They're delicious and good for you!
Yum! Yum! Don't you love to eat [green beans]?

Repeat the verse as many times as desired, substituting other healthful foods for the underlined words.

Ada Goren, Winston-Salem, NC

Ten Little Kernels

Celebrate the senses with this splendid popcorn song.

(sung to the tune of "Ten Little Indians")

One little, two little, three little kernels.
Four little, five little, six little kernels.
Seven little, eight little, nine little kernels.
Ten kernels in the bag!

Pop! Pop! Pop! Oh, what a sight!
Watch, watch, watch as they turn white!
Sniff, sniff, sniff. I want a bite!
Let's pop some today! Yea!

Merrilee Walker, Richmond, RI

Pizza, Pizza!

In *Pete's a Pizza* by William Steig, Pete feels miserable because it's raining and he can't play ball with his friends. His father cheers him up—in a most unexpected way—by transforming him into a pizza! This special recipe calls for plenty of kneading, stretching, twirling, and tickling as well as lots of love.

After reading the book aloud, encourage students to pretend to make pizzas as they sing the song below. For added fun, have each student transform a favorite stuffed toy into a pizza. Mama mia!

(sung to the tune of "The Mulberry Bush")

This is the way we pour the water, pour the yeast, pour the flour.
This is the way we mix it up to make a pizza pie.

This is the way we knead the dough, knead the dough, knead the dough.
This is the way we knead the dough to make a pizza pie.

This is the way we toss the dough, toss the dough, toss the dough.
This is the way we toss the dough to make a pizza pie.

This is the way we stretch the dough, stretch the dough, stretch the dough.
This is the way we stretch the dough to make a pizza pie.

This is the way we spread the sauce, spread the sauce, spread the sauce.
This is the way we spread the sauce to make a pizza pie.

This is the way we sprinkle the cheese, sprinkle the cheese, sprinkle the cheese.
This is the way we sprinkle the cheese to make a pizza pie.

This is the way our pizza bakes, pizza bakes, pizza bakes.
Take it out; we'll eat it up, our yummy pizza pie!

Rachel Castro
Albuquerque, NM

Cheese Pizza!

Give any pizza unit pizzazz with this tasty tune!

(sung to the tune of "Peanut Butter and Jelly")

First, you take the sauce,
And you spread it, you spread it.

Pantomime spreading sauce.

Chorus (sing twice after each verse):
Pizza, gooey pizza, with cheese!

*Pat legs for six counts; throw
hands outward, palms up.*

Then you take the cheese,
And you shred it, you shred it.

Pantomime shredding cheese.

Then you have to wait
While you bake it, you bake it.

Cross arms and tap foot.

Then you take the pizza,
And you eat it, you eat it.

Pantomime eating pizza.

Ruby Boyatzis, Green Hill International, Athens, Greece

The Pizza Song

This catchy song will have your youngsters' mouths watering for a favorite food. After singing the song once, substitute the word *cheese* in the first line with any topping your students suggest. After teaching youngsters this song, invite each child to make a mini pizza all her own by having her top a slice of Italian bread with pizza sauce and a sprinkle of cheese. Yum!

(sung to the tune of "Bingo")

There is a treat I love to eat with lots and lots of
[che-ese]—
P-I-Z-Z-A,
P-I-Z-Z-A,
P-I-Z-Z-A,
And pizza is its name—yay!

Judy Patterson
Our Hope Lutheran School
Huntertown, IN

All About Me

Personal Praise

Celebrate each child's uniqueness with this simple song. Just announce a child's name and a personality trait. Ask the special child to stand in front of the group while the class sings his praises!

(sung to the tune of "The Wheels on the Bus")

The [Alex] in our class [loves to sing,
Loves to sing, loves to sing].
The [Alex] in our class [loves to sing].
He's special that way!

I Am Special

Find out what makes each of your youngsters special with this song and activity. To begin, have youngsters sing the chorus of the song below. Then invite a child to tell what makes her feel special. Sing the second verse of the song using the child's name and her response. Repeat the activity until each child has had a turn to share a unique quality.

(sung to the tune of "Where Is Thumbkin?")

Chorus:
I am special. I am special.
I'm a star! I'm a star!
There's no one quite like me.
There's no one quite like me.
Near or far.
Near or far.

LeeAnn Collins
Sunshine House, Lansing, MI

[Ashley] is special.
[Ashley] is special.
She/He [helps her mother].
She/He [helps her mother].
There's no one like [Ashley].
There's no one like [Ashley].
Near or far.
Near or far.

Who Is Here Today?

Here's a simple song that helps youngsters learn the names of their classmates. Just include a different child's name each time you repeat the verse. Hurray!

(sung to the tune of "If You're Happy and You Know It")

Oh, [child's name] is here today. Shout hooray! Hooray!
Oh, [child's name] is here today. Shout hooray! Hooray!
Oh, [child's name] is here today.
[He/She] will learn and work and play.
Oh, [child's name] is here today. Shout hooray! Hooray!

Maria Niebruegge
Blue Ridge Elementary, Columbia, MO

So Glad You're Here!

Looking for a song that will help your youngsters learn each child's name? Invite students to sing this jazzy jingle to each child! This tune is not only great for the first days of school, it's also a wonderful way to welcome new students who arrive later in the year.

(sung to the tune of "If You're Happy and You Know It")

We're so glad to have you in our class!
  Shout child's name.
We're so glad to have you in our class!
  Shout child's name.
We're so glad you're here today!
  We will sing and learn and play!
We're so glad to have you in our class!
  Shout child's name.

Ada Goren, Winston-Salem, NC

We're All Different!

Help your youngsters understand the importance of individuality with this poem.

What kind of stew
Would beef stew be
If every vegetable
Were like a pea?

"It wouldn't be great,"
Said a carrot, "You see,
The people would miss
The color in me."

Said onion, "I flavor
With just the right touch.
If onions were peas,
Stew wouldn't be much."

"It wouldn't feed many,"
Said the potatoes with ease.
"We're bigger and much more
Filling than peas."

"It would be a disaster,"
They were all quick to agree,
"For every vegetable to be
Like a pea!"

What kind of world would our
World be
If every person were exactly
Like me?

Mary Nelson
Cedar Rapids, IA

A Salute to Siblings

This song invites youngsters to stand up for "sibling-hood." Hooray!

Stand Up for Siblings

(sung to the tune of "If You're Happy and You Know It")

If you have a big [brother/sister], stand right up.
If you have a big [brother/sister], stand right up.
Big [brothers/sisters], it's true, are older than you.
If you have a big [brother/sister], stand right up.

If you have a little [brother/sister], stand right up.
If you have a little [brother/sister], stand right up.
Little [brothers/sisters], it's true, are younger than you.
If you have a little [brother/sister], stand right up.

If you're an only child, stand right up.
If you're an only child, stand right up.
In your own family, you are special—yes sirree!
If you're an only child, stand right up.

This Friend Is My Friend

Use this simple song to introduce your youngsters to each other and to the meaning of friendship.

(sung to the tune of "This Land Is Your Land")

This friend is your friend.
This friend is my friend,
When we are working,
When we are playing.
And when I need help,
He's/She's there to help me.
[Child's name] is a friend to you and me!

Lucia Kemp Henry
Fallon, NV

Good Manners Matter!

(sung to the tune of "I'm a Little Teapot")

I have super manners. Yes, I do.
I can say, "Please," and "Thank you," too.
When I play with friends, I like to share.
That's the way I show I care!

Lori Young
Growing Tree Learning Center
Casselberry, FL

It's Time for Show and Share

Get little ones prepared to listen by singing this song before sharing time. Each time the song is sung, substitute a different child's name in the last line.

(sung to the tune of "The Farmer in the Dell")

It's time for show and share!
It's time for show and share!
Sit right down and lend an ear.
It's time for show and share!

It's time for show and share!
It's time for show and share!
Sit right down and lend an ear.
It's [child's name]'s turn to share.

Toni Osterbuhr
Price School
Wichita, KS

A Sharing Song

Need a gentle way to remind students to share? Sing this simple song!

(sung to the tune of "Looby Loo")

Sharing is nice for you.
Sharing is nice for me.
Sharing's the thing to do.
See how polite you can be!

The Sharing Song

Use this song as a gentle reminder for youngsters to share.

(sung to the tune of "Are You Sleeping?")

Are you sharing? Are you sharing?
Be a friend. Be a friend.
Sharing is caring. Caring is sharing.
Be a friend. Be a friend.

Amy Regan, Woodfern Elementary
Neshanic Station, NJ

Feelings

Lead your little ones in singing this tune about feelings. After singing the last line, make the appropriate face and invite each child to make a face that also reflects the feeling mentioned in the song.

(sung to the tune of "For He's a Jolly Good Fellow")

When I feel very [happy],
When I feel very [happy],
When I feel very [happy],
My face will look like this.

Sing additional verses, replacing the underlined word with other feeling words, such as *sad, angry, frightened,* and *sleepy.*

LeeAnn Collins, Lansing, MI

Feelings Galore!

Happy? Sad? Mad? Encourage your youngsters to talk about their feelings with this snappy song.

(sung to the tune of "Sing a Song of Sixpence")

Are you feeling happy?
Are you feeling sad?
Are you feeling quiet
Or a little mad?
Maybe you're excited—
You want to jump and shout!
There are so many feelings that
We all can talk about!

Who's the Student of the Week?

Honor each special Student of the Week with this lively song!

(sung to the tune of "Camptown Races")

Who's the Student of the Week?
[Patrick! Patrick!]

Who's the Student of the Week?
[Patrick] is the one!

He's/She's special, don't you know?

That's why we love him/her so!   *Sign "I love you."*

Who's the Student of the Week?
[Patrick] is the one!

Maureen Arbour
St. Dunstan School
Brighton, MI

Kindergarten Explorers

This song is a great boost to encourage your youngsters to use dramatic play to explore the world and their places in it.

(sung to the tune of "I've Been Working on the Railroad")

I'm a kindergarten explorer
Exploring every day.
I'm a kindergarten explorer
And I have a dream today.
When I'm working or I'm playing
And pretending what I'll be,
I'm a kindergarten explorer.
Exploring to be me!

Debbie Pinheiro, Northbridge Primary School, Whitinsville, MA

Eyes, Ears, Nose, and Mouth

Help youngsters tune in to body parts with this song!

(sung to the tune of "Row, Row, Row Your Boat")

Eyes, ears, nose, and mouth.
These are parts of me!
Arms and legs and elbows too!
And don't forget my knee!

Deborah Garmon, Groton, CT

The Birthdate Song

Here's a fun way to review birthdays. Write each child's name and birthdate on a paper plate. Seat your students in a circle. Toss a plate into the center; then sing the song below. Vary the activity to practice addresses.

(sung to the tune of "If You're Happy and You Know It")

If your birthdate's on the plate, pick it up.
If your birthdate's on the plate, pick it up.
If your birthdate's on the plate, then we think
    you're really great!
If your birthdate's on the plate, pick it up.

Wendy Anderson
Mt. Juliet Elementary
Mt. Juliet, TN

Here We Go Round the Birthday Cake

This personalized birthday song will have your little ones huffing, puffing, and giggling! During a group time, lead children in circling around the birthday boy or girl as they sing the first verse of the following song. Then have them circle around in the opposite direction as they sing the second verse. Invite the honoree to pretend to blow out the "candles" (her classmates). Youngsters will giggle with delight as they fall to the floor!

(sung to the tune of "The Mulberry Bush")

Here we go round the birthday cake, the birthday cake, the birthday cake.
Here we go round the birthday cake.
Today is [child's name]'s birthday!

Make a wish and blow us out, blow us out, blow us out.
Make a wish and blow us out.
Today is [child's name]'s birthday!

Karen Eiben and Melinda Wilson, The Kid's Place Child Development Center
LaSalle, IL

Birthday Whoop-De-Do!

Have a birthday to celebrate? Then start the day out on a happy note with this birthday song. In advance personalize a party horn for each child. During a group time, give each child a horn; then invite the birthday child to stand in front of the class. Lead your little ones in singing the following song; then have them blow their horns at the end of the song. Collect the horns; then store them in a gift-wrapped box for use during future birthday celebrations.

Today's a Special Day

(sung to the tune of "Head and Shoulders")

Today's a special day for you.
Just for you!
Today's a special day for you.
Just for you!
You're one year older.
Whoop-de, whoop-de-do!
Happy birthday!
Hooray for you!
Whoop-de-do!   *Blow horn.*

Lisa Leonardi
Norfolk, MA

Telephone Number Song

Memorizing a telephone number is a cinch with this quick little ditty! Simply substitute each youngster's telephone number and name in the verse below; then sing, sing, r-r-ring!

(sung to the tune of "London Bridge")

[123-4567], ring, ring, ring, ring, ring, ring.
[123-4567] is [Kent's] telephone number!

LeeAnn Stroud
Fountain Lake Elementary
Hot Springs, AR

What's Your Number?

Here's a tune to help youngsters review their phone numbers. Before singing, give each child a card with her phone number on it. If she can't remember her number when it's her turn to answer, she can refer to the card.

(sung to the tune of "Mary Had a Little Lamb")

Please tell us your phone number,
Phone number, phone number.
Please tell us your phone number.
[Child's name], tell us please.

adapted from a song by Michele Tunstall
Cambria County Christian School, Johnstown, PA

The Shoe-Tying Song

Teach your students this catchy song, and not only will there be lots of singing going on, but lots of shoe tying too!

(sung to the tune of "The Mulberry Bush")

This is the way we tie our shoes, tie our shoes, tie our shoes.
This is the way we tie our shoes in kindergarten.

Take the ends and cross the laces, cross the laces, cross the laces.
Take the ends and cross the laces, as we tie our shoes.

Take one lace and loop it through, loop it through, loop it through.
Take one lace and loop it through, as we tie our shoes.

Next, you pull the laces down, laces down, laces down.
Next, you pull the laces down, as we tie our shoes.

With one lace we make a loop, make a loop, make a loop.
With one lace we make a loop, as we tie our shoes.

Take one lace and wrap it around, wrap it around, wrap it around.
Take one lace and wrap it around, as we tie our shoes.

Grab the tip and pull it through, pull it through, pull it through.
Grab the tip and pull it through, as we tie our shoes.

Then we have to pull them tight, pull them tight, pull them tight.
Then we have to pull them tight; we can tie our shoes!

Pamela Kilrain, Helotes Elementary, Helotes, TX

Weather

What's the Weather?

Have youngsters sing this short tune during each day's opening activities. Then invite your calendar helper or another volunteer to answer the question at the end of the song.

(sung to the tune of "Jingle Bells")

Sunny day,
Cloudy day,
Or rainy day so gray?
Look outside and tell us now:
Can we go out to play?
(Repeat verse.)

Betty Silkunas
Lansdale, PA

Windy Weather!

Youngsters can't see the wind, but they are reminded of its presence with this breezy poem!

The wind sees you as it blows through town,
Singing in your ears with a whistling sound.
But can you see the wind? It's sneaky and fast!
It messes up your hair as it breezes past.

Rain and Thunder

(sung to the tune of "Are You Sleeping?")

Rain and thunder.
Rain and thunder.
Boom! Boom! Boom!
Boom! Boom! Boom!
See the flash of lightning.
Oh, my gosh, it's frightening!
Boom! Boom! Boom!
Boom! Boom! Boom!

Marisa Ellin, An Even Start in Newport, Newport, RI

I've Been Listening to the Rainfall

(sung to the tune of "I've Been Working on the Railroad")

I've been listening to the rainfall,
All the morning long.
I've been listening to the rainfall,
As I sing this little song.
Can't you hear the wind a-blowing,
Rustling through the trees?
Can't you hear the thunder rumbling?
Now sing this song with me.

Come out, Mr. Sun. Come out, Mr. Sun.
Come out, Mr. Sun, today and stay!
Come out, Mr. Sun. Come out, Mr. Sun.
So we can go out and play!

Melissa Pyles
Carter St. Headstart of Childhood Development Services
Inverness, FL

Out Pop the Raindrops!

(sung to the tune of "Pop! Goes the Weasel")

All around the sky today,
The clouds are full of raindrops.
They push and shove until they burst.
Out pop the raindrops!

Patricia Moeser
University of Wisconsin Preschool Laboratory
Madison, WI

Moving in the Weather

Get the wiggles out with this song that will have your little ones moving and singing about weather. Then use the song's pattern as a springboard for creating additional verses with different motions.

(sung to the tune of "Mary Had a Little Lamb")

We are hopping in the snow,
In the snow, in the snow.
We are hopping in the snow
And clapping as we go.

We are running in the wind,
In the wind, in the wind.
We are running in the wind
And laughing as we go.

We are marching in the rain,
In the rain, in the rain.
We are marching in the rain
And splashing as we go.

We are skipping in the sun,
In the sun, in the sun.
We are skipping in the sun
And waving as we go.

Debbie Korytoski
Ellerslie, GA

Blowing in the Wind

Blow some blustery action into your wind studies with this movement song. First write the song on a sheet of chart paper. Sing the song, encouraging students to sing along as well as act out the movement of the blowing object. Repeat the song, each time replacing the underlined words with one of the following: a big tree, our school flag, a weather vane, a windmill.

The Wind Blows...

(sung to the tune of "The Wheels on the Bus")

The wind blows [a feather] just like this,
Just like this, just like this.
The wind blows [a feather] just like this,
All through the day.

Waiting For A Sunny Day

(sung to the tune of "This Old Man")

Drip, drop, drop. Drip, drop, drop.
Will these raindrops ever stop?
I guess we'll wait for another sunny day.
Then we'll go outside to play!

Deborah Garmon, Groton, CT

Little Rain Cloud

Stay dry with this soothing springtime poem.

I see a little rain cloud

Floating in the sky.

I see a little rain cloud

Slowly rolling by.

It rains upon the housetops.

It rains upon the trees.

It rains on my umbrella.

But it doesn't rain on me!

LeeAnn Collins
Mason, MI

Transportation

Stop and Go

Teach your youngsters a little traffic safety using this catchy verse.

Red on top
Means stop.
Yellow in between:

Stay and wait for green.
Green below:
Let's go!

Diane Leschak-Halverson
Nashwauk-Keewatin ECFE, Keewatin, MN

Where Is Red Light?

Red, yellow, green—what do all those lights mean? Help little ones figure out traffic signals with this song. Tape a craft stick handle to each of three paper circles— one red, one yellow, and one green. Ask three children to hold these light puppets up high during the appropriate parts of the song.

(sung to the tune of "Where is Thumbkin?")

Where is red light? Where is red light?
Here I am. Here I am.
Tell us what you say, sir. Tell us what you say, sir.
I say stop! I say stop!

Where is yellow light? Where is yellow light?
Here I am. Here I am.
Tell us what you say, sir. Tell us what you say, sir.
I say wait! I say wait!

Where is green light? Where is green light?
Here I am. Here I am.
Tell us what you say, sir. Tell us what you say, sir.
I say go! I say go!

Red says stop, yellow says wait,
Green says go, green says go.
These are traffic signals, these are traffic signals
That we know, that we know.

Debbie Korytoski, Ellerslie, GA

Five Fast Racecars

To prepare for this action poem, label five paper plates (steering wheels), each with a different number from 1 to 5. Provide five students each with a different steering wheel. Invite the students to stand in front of the class; then watch those five fast race cars go!

Five fast racecars speeding round the track.

The first car said, "I can't look back!"

The second car said, "Oh, no! I'm out of gas!"

The third car said, "Beep! Beep! I'm fast!"

The fourth car said, "Watch my tires spin."

The fifth car said, "Vroom, vroom. I win!"

Then beep went a horn and flash went the lights,

And five fast racecars sped out of sight!

Angela Neimann
J. F. Burns Elementary
Kings Mills, OH

Index

191

192